Transforming Your Kitchen
with Stock Cabinetry

Transforming Your Kitchen with Stock Cabinetry

Design, Select, and Install
for a Custom Look
at the Right Price

JONATHAN & SHERRY BENSON

FOX CHAPEL
PUBLISHING

DEDICATION

This book is dedicated to our parents and children.

ACKOWLEDGEMENTS

We would like to thank Doug Hicks for his tireless efforts editing this book. We would also like to thank all of the staff at Fox Chapel for working so hard to bring this book to life. Thanks also to Kevan Stratton for helping to install the kitchen cabinets in our subject kitchen.

This book would not have been possible without the patience of the following homeowners who were so generous in letting us invade and photograph their wonderful kitchens: Jeff Benson and Margaret Elbert, Mary Kate Murray and Greg Couch, and Tina Fruchter.

We would also like to acknowledge the following manufacturers for letting us provide images of their products without any restrictions:

- Crown Point Cabinetry
- Diamond Cabinets
- Granite Transformations
- KraftMaid Cabinetry
- Quality Custom Cabinets Inc.
- Trueform Concrete
- Wood-Mode

Photos on pages 16, 18, 20, 22, 24, 26, 28, 30, 32, 34, and 36 courtesy of Diamond Cabinets.
Photos on page 77 courtesy of Masco Retail Cabinet Group, manufacturers of KraftMaid Cabinetry.
Photos on pages 81 and 84 courtesy of Quality Custom Cabinets Inc.
Photo on page 83 (left) courtesy of Wood-Mode Fine Custom Cabinetry.
Photo on page 83 (right) courtesy of Crown Point Cabinetry.
Photo on page 138 courtesy of Granite Transformations.
Photo on page 143 courtesy of Trueform Concrete, *www.trueformconcrete.com*.
Photos/illustrations on pages 79, 81, 82, 83, 85, 118, 127, and 140 previously published by and reproduced under license with Direct Holdings Americas Inc.

ISBN 978-1-56523-395-9
Library of Congress Cataloging-in-Publication Data

Benson, Jonathan.
    Transforming your kitchen with stock cabinetry / by Jonathan and Sherry Benson.
        p. cm.
    Includes index.
    ISBN 978-1-56523-395-9
    1. Kitchen cabinets. I. Benson, Sherry. II. Title.
    TT197.5.K57B46 2010
    684.1'6--dc22
                                    2009051971

To learn more about the other great books from Fox Chapel Publishing, or to find a retailer near you, call toll-free 800-457-9112 or visit us at *www.FoxChapelPublishing.com*.

Note to Authors: We are always looking for talented authors to write new books in our areas of woodworking, design, and related crafts. Please send a brief letter describing your idea to Acquisition Editor, 1970 Broad Street, East Petersburg, PA 17520.

Printed in China
First Printing: June 2010

Contents

What You Can Learn From This Book

PAGES

15–37

More than just pretty pictures, this kitchen gallery features helpful commentary from our author and his wife. He's a professional cabinetmaker. She's an executive chef. Together, they will discuss the design and functionality of over 10 gorgeous stock cabinet kitchens.

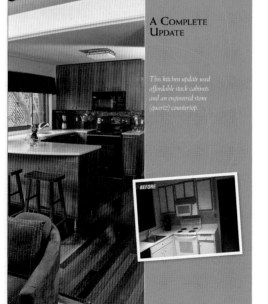

PAGES

40–57

Read about real homeowners who have been through the renovation process. You'll learn about the design challenges they faced and how affordable stock cabinetry provided the solutions.

Introduction

If you are reading this book, you are most likely dissatisfied with your current kitchen. You have probably seen many beautiful kitchens in show homes, magazines, and books. And this book is no exception. Within this book, you will see many photos of attractive and stylish kitchens. However, there is one important difference. The kitchens featured in this book have all been outfitted with affordable stock cabinets that can be purchased from a local home improvement center and installed yourself. The result is that you save lots of money and end up with a fabulous—but affordable—kitchen.

In the following pages, you will see the many styles that can be achieved with stock cabinets. You'll also meet several homeowners who have been through the renovation process and used stock cabinetry to achieve their goals. You'll see their gorgeous results and learn how they did it. You'll also find the story of a kitchen I recently re-built in my own home using stock cabinets. I think the finished product is beautiful, and it functions as well as it looks.

Before we go much farther, let me introduce myself. My friends call me Jon, and I am a cabinet and furniture maker. I have been involved in

This is the kitchen author Jonathan Benson created in his own home using stock cabinetry. Step-by-step installation instructions beginning on page 106.

many new and remodeled kitchen projects over the years. I am also a licensed general contractor. In addition, I have even had experience owning a restaurant and seeing many of the special needs of a restaurant kitchen—speed, efficiency, and the wise use of space. Many of these ideas can be used to create a better home kitchen. So for this book, I have also solicited the expert assistance of my wife, Executive Chef Sherry Benson. She will be inserting her thoughts and comments in some boxes that we'll call *Restaurant Lessons from a Pro*.

Designing and installing a new kitchen can be a complex yet very rewarding project. Today's kitchen is not just a factory for the production of meals. It is often the family gathering place, the drop-off point for school backpacks and mail, the location for entertaining guests, the communications center where family members describe their day as they prepare the evening meal, and a place for solace and quiet at the beginning or ending of the day. So it is worth it to take some time to decide exactly what you want in your kitchen even before you call a designer, contact a contractor, or begin the job yourself. I hope this book will help you achieve that.

—Jonathan Benson

Author Jonathan Benson and his wife, Sherry, selecting their preferred tools of the trade to slice a loaf of bread. In her feature, *Restaurant Lessons from a Pro*, Sherry provides insider tips for creating an organized and efficient kitchen.

Shaping Your New Kitchen

❏ **What activities do I want to happen in my kitchen?**
   - ❏ Cooking meals?
   - ❏ Eating in? (If so, for how many people?)
   - ❏ Baking?
   - ❏ Canning fruits and vegetables?
   - ❏ Gatherings? (Central meeting place?)
   - ❏ Entertaining?
   - ❏ Paying bills/use as an office?
   - ❏ Conducting hobbies and crafts?
   - ❏ Working on children's homework?
   - ❏ Organizing family events?
   - ❏ Conducting other activities besides cooking?

❏ **Do I like to prepare gourmet meals? Alternatively, am I looking for a place to prepare three quick family meals a day and snacks? (Or both?)**

❏ **Does my kitchen have to be a place to prepare large meals (i.e. holiday gatherings, dinner parties, etc.) on a regular basis?**

❏ **How many people will be working in the kitchen at one time?**

❏ **Does there need to be a food pantry?**

❏ **How often do I shop and how much food do I need to be able to store between trips to the grocery store?**

❏ **Does anyone in my house who will be preparing meals or eating in the kitchen have special needs (disabled, special height requirements, etc.)?**

❏ **What needs to be stored in the kitchen in addition to the food itself?**
   - ❏ Fine china?
   - ❏ Table linens?
   - ❏ Glassware?
   - ❏ Utensils?
   - ❏ Cooking supplies (pots, pans, etc.)?
   - ❏ Wine collection?
   - ❏ Cookbooks?
   - ❏ Small countertop appliances?

❏ **Do I like the look and functionality of a center island or do I want space that is more open?**

❏ **Would my family and friends sit at a snack bar?**

❏ **Do I want a wine or wet bar?**

❏ **Do I want my kitchen to be a decorative showplace in the house?**

❏ **Do I want my kitchen to fit in with the rest of the house (i.e. traditional style, contemporary, etc.) or is it okay to be an independent environment?**

❏ **How much space do I have available in my current kitchen? Could I get more space by removing walls or completely rearranging the location of appliances and use areas?**

❏ **Can electric or plumbing lines be moved? Is there basement access below the kitchen for utility lines?**

CHAPTER 1

Inspiration Gallery

A he says/she says perspective on stock cabinet kitchens from author Jonathan Benson and his wife, executive chef Sherry Benson.

Kitchens come in all sizes and shapes. You will probably never find one the same size as yours, but you can draw inspiration for yours by looking at photos of others. In this chapter, we have pulled together photos of some of the better home kitchens we have seen built using affordable stock cabinets.

My wife, Sherry, and I sat down and studied each photo carefully. Then, drawing on our experiences working in both home and restaurant kitchens, we have added our comments. We looked at practicality as well as easily overlooked design details. We hope you get some ideas you can use in your new kitchen.

WINDHAM MAPLE

SHERRY SAYS:

This is a great kitchen for frequent entertainers. Lots of things can be going on at the same time, with mom or dad at the desk on the computer ①, kids doing homework on the island, and the cook, along with one or even two helpers, getting the family dinner ready.

This kitchen is set up to allow three work triangles. (For more about the Kitchen Work Triangle, see page 64.) On the left side in the background, the refrigerator-sink-stove triangle is sufficient to create a complete meal ②, while the right-hand side can function as a baking station ③, with the oven easily accessible and two sinks nearby. The dishwasher is not visible, but is in the island next to the sink ④. This would allow easy cleanup, and plenty of nearby storage allows easy access to dish storage. This station is also well suited as a prep station ⑤, with a refrigerator in close range and a sink for wash-up. The symmetry of the kitchen is visually appealing and the muted colors are calming.

JON SAYS:

This kitchen has a nice balance of traditional and contemporary styles. The cathedral ceiling gives the space an open feeling.

I like having a desk with storage shelves off to the side because books, mail, and papers piled on the island make it difficult to work or eat there. This is a very light and airy space and has a very symmetrical balance. Notice how most of the shapes balance off the center. I really like the contemporary fan hood ⑥ centered over the stove. It seems to fit in well, even though the cabinets themselves are more traditional in style.

There is a lot of counter space in this kitchen, which could be very expensive if you plan to use stone. One option is to use stone only for the island, which has a rounded edge, and use a less expensive material for the counters.

Photo courtesy of Diamond Cabinets.

SHILOH MAPLE

SHERRY SAYS:

I love the windows and the brightness of this kitchen, although a bit more color would be appealing. The work triangle is not obvious in this kitchen as the refrigerator is not shown.

I would have put the main sink in the corner in front of the window, but if the view were too nice, I would never get around to cooking! This is also a comfortable kitchen to work in, with the work stool and the wood floors ①. Jon would love the trees and the wood in this kitchen. He would also love that a beautiful kitchen comes without the expense of stone. Because of the kitchen's subdued look and feel, good quality laminate countertops could fit beautifully here without making it look cheap.

JON SAYS:

I do love the wood and the trees, and it is true, I am mindful of budgets. With the sink in the island and if the refrigerator was just off to the left, it would create a good work triangle. The island's wood butcher-block top ② is great, right in the middle of the kitchen where most work takes place.

This kitchen does have a nice open feel and the windows bring in a lot of light. The tile backsplash ③ brings in some detail, but I agree that more color would be nice. In addition, of interest, not all of the handles always have to match. You can purchase white cabinets like these for not a lot of money and then dress them up with nice crown molding ④ and turned legs on the island.

Photo courtesy of Diamond Cabinets.

BRADSHAWE RUSTIC ALDER

SHERRY SAYS:

Forget functionality. This is the kitchen I want when the kids leave the nest, and Jon and I can have romantic dinners, or at least wine and cheese. The dark cabinets and appliances give it a warm, even romantic touch, while the lighter cabinets keep it from being oppressively dark.

The wooden ceiling ① adds a natural, almost intimate, feeling to the space. Everything in here seems to evoke a bygone era, with the exception of the appliances, which are downplayed by color or covered by cabinetry, like the stove exhaust hood ②.

All I would want to add is a fireplace. *And champagne.*

JON SAYS:

I absolutely agree. It is a date. This room does have the feel of a comfortable den and it would be relaxing to spend time here with you. I also like having access to the outside right off the kitchen ③, so we can cook together when I am grilling part of the meal.

Different countertops work well in this kitchen, meaning you could get by with something less expensive on the counters, but a nice stone top on the island ④ would give the kitchen its best look, as everything else in the kitchen seems to draw you to it as a focal point. Keeping the island top simple, with no bevels, angles, or rounding would minimize finishing costs for the stone.

Photo courtesy of Diamond Cabinets.

MONTEREY MAPLE 1

SHERRY SAYS:

I love the display space at the top of the cabinets and the natural color of the wood. The rack above the stovetop ① is a great feature for easy access of seasonings, dishes, or storage/cooling of baked goods, as shown here.

I think this kitchen is a great example of contrast between old and new, natural and manufactured, and dark and light. Not a big space, but nicely done. Love the stove!

JON SAYS:

This is one of the few examples in this book of display cabinets ② above the upper cabinets. This is a great way to utilize this space and display precious items not used daily.

There are warming lights in the exhaust hood ③ that help to keep prepared foods hot until they are ready to serve. Note the hanging lights ④ right above the island that can bring light in right when you need it. Also notice the combination of black and white countertops.

This would be a good design for a small kitchen as the dishwasher is located under the island. You cannot see it in this photo, but the cabinets extend out into the dining room, which is a great way to add more storage space without increasing the actual size of the kitchen.

This stove ⑤ might have cost as much as the cabinets, but this is where the priorities were here. I believe this would be Sherry's preference as well.

Photo courtesy of Diamond Cabinets.

AURORA OAK

SHERRY SAYS:

I love the hearth feature in the range area ①. It gives the kitchen a warm and inviting look. The hearth is beautiful, but the space is made more functional with a faucet for pots ②, a rack for utensils ③, and a shelf for seasonings ④. The island has a component not usually seen in islands, glass doors ⑤, which could be used to showcase attractive crystal, china, or collectibles. One thing to note with islands is to plan how you will use the space so you are sure to include sufficient lighting and electrical outlets in the right places. The bay window ⑥ would be the perfect place to grow some herbs for the kitchen, and that view would keep Jon occupied while he does the dishes.

JON SAYS:

This looks like a good use of the available space. Notice how the 45° angle theme created by the corner range is repeated in the island and counter in the foreground ⑦. This helps give the design unity and interest. It is also a good idea to have a smaller prep sink in the island and keep the larger sink and dirty dishes off to the side. The bay window also adds a nice touch and helps to capitalize on the stunning view. Be sure to use tempered glass on low glass doors such as those on the island for safety.

Photo courtesy of Diamond Cabinets.

SULLIVAN CHERRY

SHERRY SAYS:

This would be a great kitchen for parents, with space for the kids to do homework, paint, or draw at the table, or play on the floor in the eating area. In the meantime, parents can work in the kitchen, which is big enough to hold more than one cook.

The raised dishwasher ① saves the user's back for picking up kids instead of dishes, and makes it harder for toddlers and pets to get into the dirty dishes. The microwave/vent hood ② also is out of little hands' reach, saves space, and is convenient for time-saving foods like frozen microwaveable vegetables. It may be a less-expensive way to go because you are buying two items in one, instead of two separate items. The combination unit is also the type of appliance you can often pick up on clearance.

JON SAYS:

This kitchen combines elements of universal design such as a raised dishwasher, a lower countertop ③ for working while seated, and plenty of room to maneuver a wheelchair.

The raised part of the island ④ also helps to create some separation between the rooms while maintaining an open feel. These stock cabinets have no shelving or soffits above, which is a good way to save money.

Photo courtesy of Diamond Cabinets.

BAYPORT CHERRY

SHERRY SAYS:

For the size of this kitchen, the work triangle is tight, making it a very efficient use of space, allowing for a lot of cooking with just a few steps from the cook. The stone island top ① provides space to make pastries in the work triangle. This is a good setup for a cook who likes to do all of the cooking themselves, but still likes some company nearby—but out of the way.

The decorative vent hood cover ② is a nice focal point, and the owners made a nice display area above the cabinets, thereby avoiding dead space.

The rug ③ gives the kitchen a homey feel, but would not stay clean for 5 minutes in my kitchen. Also make sure any rugs or mats you place in your kitchen are secure, and the flooring is slip-resistant to avoid falls.

JON SAYS:

The refrigerator door ④, which is the wood paneled door just off to the left of center, could open across the doorway to the right. We lived in a house with this configuration and the traffic jam drove us crazy. Always consider the traffic flow through the kitchen when placing appliances. The layout of this kitchen may have worked better by placing the refrigerator a little farther to the left- or on the right-hand side of the kitchen.

Sherry speaks with experience about falls in the kitchen.

Photo courtesy of Diamond Cabinets.

BRITTANY OAK

SHERRY SAYS:

This warm, inviting kitchen seems as much like a library as a kitchen, except with fewer books. (The kitchen and library are my favorite rooms in any house!) The sink in the island creates a work triangle in an otherwise linear galley-style kitchen. The exhaust hood ① is an elegant focal point, as is the island. Drawers next to the stove provide easy access to pans, and the under-the-counter-level sinks ② add to the subtle look of the kitchen.

I love the bookshelf on the end of the island, which is something I have always wanted (that's a hint, Jon!) One thing that concerns me is the detail on the island top corners. If there were a lot of activity or quick movement in this kitchen, the protrusions would be easy to bump up against, and could cause bruising or damage.

JON SAYS:

I will get right to work on that bookshelf. This might be a good place to add a few more layout basics. Notice the placement of the stove and refrigerator. There should always be a cabinet ③ between them, as is the case here. It may be tempting to place them next to each other, but this can waste a lot of energy as these appliances work against each other.

Notice the location of the television ④, an often-overlooked item when designing a kitchen. An unplanned TV usually ends up somewhere that causes a loss of valuable counter space. It will need wiring for cable and possibly a space for a cable box. So, if you are planning to have a TV in the kitchen, think ahead. Doors called flipper doors that slide back out of the way are an excellent way to keep it out of sight when not in use.

I always like tall cabinets such as these ⑤ to make the best use of available space. I sometimes add a slot in one of the lower cabinets for a short library ladder that can be pulled out when needed.

Photo courtesy of Diamond Cabinets.

SELENA MAPLE

SHERRY SAYS:

What a kitchen! Too many cooks may spoil a stew, but you will not have any problem fitting them in this kitchen. Of course, this kitchen is much bigger than most of us will ever have, but you can adapt the features in smaller kitchens.

The different angles on the island each provide a space for different workstations. The double windows add brightness and create a space for growing herbs and flowers, for cooking and beauty. The placement of the dishwasher ① is ideal because it is located (next to the sink) close to storage and use areas, making cleanup more efficient. I also love the convenient plate rack ② on the upper-right-hand cabinet, although it might get a bit too dirty in my kitchen. The sink on the left ③ would make a wonderful bar area, especially with a nice-sized wine rack nearby. This is a great family space, and a great entertaining space as the open layout allows easy transition between the kitchen and the living space. The upper display case ④ near the center of the picture helps with the transition between the kitchen and the living area.

JON SAYS:

I agree: *"What a kitchen!"* Cabinets that extend almost to the ceiling ⑤ can create a shadow around the top, which adds drama to the design. The wood flooring and wall and trim colors carried through to the living room creates unity between the two rooms.

Finally, the cook top in the island ⑥ allows the cook to stay in the action and communicate with everyone, even with those in the living room. Ways to reduce costs for a kitchen like this include having less expensive countertops; a range, rather than a cook top and separate oven; and open shelving, rather than cabinets with glass doors. I will pick out a bottle of wine and let's get started cooking!

Photo courtesy of Diamond Cabinets.

MONTGOMERY MAPLE

SHERRY SAYS:

Talk about bright—this kitchen will open your eyes in the morning! It also has some features that I really like, including a large window above the sink, many display cabinets, and a floating island ①. I also like that the island has a built-in cutting board, which can really come in handy.

Even better are the extra upper cabinets ② on the back wall. Cabinets like these add an incredible amount of extra storage for infrequently used items, like pasta machines or seasonal dishware. On the other wall, the symmetric upper cabinets with added detail are a beautiful focal point. The little drawers ③ on the bottom of these cabinets are useful for smaller items, like spices and yeast that might otherwise cause clutter.

JON SAYS:

It sounds as if you are ready to get started right away on this one. There might actually be enough storage for all of your cooking supplies. The floating island is a good feature and this can be a good way to save money and make cleaning easier. Adding a table and chairs completes the kitchen's eat-in function.

The lighting inside the cabinets ④ is a great way to brighten things.

Photo courtesy of Diamond Cabinets.

LAURELDALE MAPLE

SHERRY SAYS:

This is a nice example of design for a small kitchen. The bar and stool ① give the cook a place to sit, or provide an out-of-the-way sitting area for company.

The counter-depth refrigerator maximizes limited floor space, and the microwave ② allows easy access by the cook and others. The shelving above the microwave ③ not only provides display space, but also includes cubbies for organizing clutter.

Cabinets that open to the dining area ④ create space for dishes and tableware.

JON SAYS:

This is a good way to make use of a small space. The shelving in place of cabinets next to the refrigerator is a good way to save money. This design has a nice tight work triangle that helps direct the food out of the refrigerator, to the stove and out to the eating area. The sink ⑤ is the first stop for the dishes returning from the table.

When you have a small space, try to make the most out of it. If you get the best quality products you can afford, pay attention to detail, and make the best use of space, you will get the best return on your investment, and can even turn the disadvantage of a smaller space into the advantage of an efficient, compact, and highly workable kitchen.

Photo courtesy of Diamond Cabinets.

CHAPTER 2

Stock Cabinet Kitchen Transformations

Two Homeowners Share Their Renovation Experiences

Stock cabinets can be a great choice for a total renovation no matter what size your kitchen. In this chapter, you will find two examples. The first is a total transformation done in a tiny Manhattan kitchen that is barely over 100 square feet in size. Maximum efficiency and storage space was of utmost importance here.

The second kitchen is an average size kitchen. The complete update includes cherry cabinets, brand new appliances, a Silestone countertop, and a fantastic Brazilian cherry floor. Again, efficiency was important, but attention to detail and a brand new look make this kitchen a joy to work and entertain in.

The one thing both kitchens have in common is their easy-to-install and reasonably priced stock cabinets.

MANHATTAN MAKEOVER

A small Manhattan kitchen is transformed with stock cabinetry and good design.

The former kitchen was dreary and lacked necessary storage space.

THE STORY

Tina Fruchter is a busy New Yorker with a great downtown apartment. Unfortunately, her small kitchen was cramped, cluttered, and drab. It did not match the rest of her stylish home or her vivacious personality. The poor layout made it difficult to cook and entertain her frequent out-of-town guests.

When it was time to remodel, Tina wanted to make her kitchen more efficient and attractive, and at the same time, do it on a budget. She worked with a local home improvement store on the design, purchased stock cabinets, and had a private contractor do the installation work.

Unfortunately, there was no room to expand. Enlarging the size of the kitchen would have required moving walls and utilities, which Tina's co-op association would not allow. Therefore, her remodel was limited to the original size of the L-shaped kitchen—just over 100 square feet.

To solve her problems, Tina designed a hard working yet attractive kitchen that made use of every inch of available space. By reconfiguring the layout, she created a more efficient and comfortable work area. The overall organization was improved with the addition of a new pantry and pull-out cabinetry.

THE GOALS

① **Improve Functionality:** Reconfigure the work triangle to create a more efficient floor plan.

② **Increase Storage:** Add cabinets and storage solutions to eliminate clutter.

③ **Make the Room More Attractive:** Use bright colors, high-end appliances, and granite countertops to create a modern yet welcoming environment.

THE PLAN

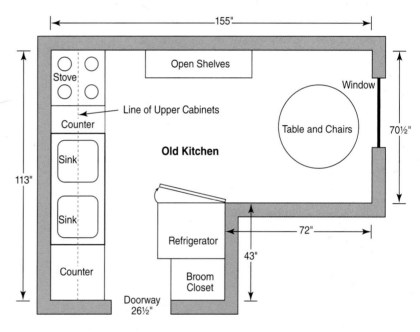

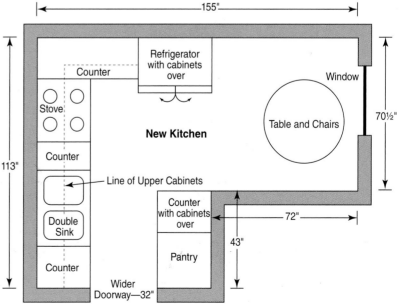

① IMPROVE FUNCTIONALITY

The former kitchen's inefficient layout disrupted the work triangle. When working at the sink or stove, opening the refrigerator required the cook to turn around. The layout problems would amplify if other cooks worked in the kitchen at the same time. The new arrangement allows for two cooks and even a standing dinner guest or two to move comfortably about the kitchen.

Move the Fridge

The original refrigerator was a typical depth but was set right at the corner of the L, and therefore made the room seem very cramped. By replacing it with a shallower counter-depth refrigerator and moving it to the other side of the room, the kitchen opened up.

Move the Stove

The outside of the L shape had wasted space where the oven door opened right against a wall. By moving the stove over, more counter and cabinet space was created. Now, pots, pans, and other items that are used daily are easy to access.

THE RESULT

With the refrigerator and the stove moved, the work triangle is now intact. The cook can easily reach everything she might need and set it conveniently on the counter. The new arrangement creates three places where someone can stand and chop or mix without having to move out of the way of the refrigerator door.

Small work areas for food preparation are on either side of the new sink.

A new work surface was created by adding upper and lower cabinets where the refrigerator used to be.

Moving the stove created this valuable counter.

ADD LIGHTING

Good lighting is essential in the kitchen and an important aspect of any remodel. For her kitchen, Tina chose stylish track lighting to illuminate the room and supplemented that with under-cabinet task lights. She also created a focal point by incorporating a ceiling fan with a decorative light fixture in the dining area.

The track lighting serves double duty. It sheds light on the entire kitchen and also adds a punch of style to the room.

Under cabinet task lighting was added throughout the kitchen.

This attractive light fixture creates an inviting atmosphere and helps to designate the dining area.

Storage is no longer an issue with abundant cabinetry in the attractive and hard-working new kitchen.

② INCREASE STORAGE

BEFORE

PULLOUTS

In the former kitchen, inexpensive open shelving filled in for the absence of wall cabinets. The cluttered kitchen wasted space from the floor to the ceiling. Today, dry goods are neatly stored in handy pullout cabinets.

Eliminating an underutilized broom closet opened up space for a floor-to-ceiling pantry cabinet that is the highlight of the new kitchen. It has six movable full-extension trays that allow for easy adjustment of the layout to match the food on-hand.

Spices and cooking oils are now neatly organized and conveniently located for cooking with this affordable rollout shelf to the left of the stove.

Every bit of space is used in this kitchen as seen with the clever pullout pot rack featured in this photograph.

CLOSE UP ON CABINETS

Storage space was at a premium in the old kitchen, but not anymore. The changes more than doubled the useful cubic feet of storage space.

The new light-colored cabinets with frosted ribbed glass panels increase the feeling of openness in this small kitchen. The cove molding around the top of the cabinets adds architectural interest and ties in well with the other moldings in the rest of the apartment.

The frosted glass on the upper cabinets allow you to vaguely see what is inside without contributing to visual clutter.

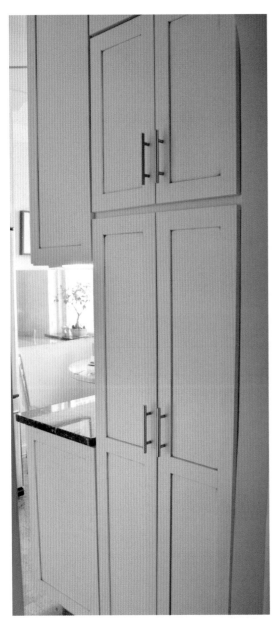

This new pantry unit more than doubles the space for food and other goods.

The refrigerator handles dictated the simple rod-style handles throughout the kitchen, including these on the cabinets.

③ MAKE THE ROOM MORE ATTRACTIVE

The old kitchen was cramped and not conducive to dining. Today, the kitchen is a welcoming place to prepare and share meals.

DESIGN PALETTE

For her design palette, Tina chose a fresh apple green and crisp white anchored with gray and black. The result is a look that is vibrant, modern, and welcoming.

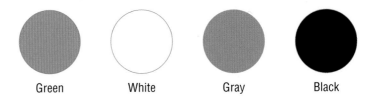

Green   White   Gray   Black

A green backsplash made from Italian glass tile adds a splash of bold color to the room.

Crisp white cabinetry creates a clean look in the new kitchen.

High-end stainless steel appliances anchor the room and add a flair of sophistication.

Black granite countertops with green flecks tie the look together.

THE AFTER

Tina loves her new kitchen. Using stock cabinets worked well and cost one-third the price of custom cabinets. The renovations more than doubled the counter space and made it a pleasure to have two or even three people working in the kitchen at the same time.

It would have been desirable to add a dishwasher, but because of plumbing issues in this older building, the co-op association does not allow installation of dishwashers at present. Nevertheless, appropriate plumbing was roughed in and the drawer cabinet to the left of the sink is the correct size for a dishwasher.

The only serious mistake made in the remodeling project was failing to tell the electrician about the desire for under-cabinet lighting during the rough-in. As a result, the newly finished walls had to be re-opened after hanging the cabinets. It was a good reminder as to why it is important to line up all of the subcontractor jobs in the correct order before beginning a remodeling job.

Finally, the job is not quite finished. There is a breakfast nook with a window and a round table with chairs at the long end of the L. Plans call for installation of a custom-built booth in the space.

A COMPLETE UPDATE

This kitchen update used affordable stock cabinets and an engineered stone (quartz) countertop.

BEFORE

THE STORY

When Greg Couch and Mary Kate Murray acquired their home, they knew they had their work cut out for them. Though they liked the general layout of the kitchen and the locations of the appliances, they described the kitchen (as well as the whole house) as having a "very '80s *Miami Vice* color scheme and feel."

The adjacent family room had textured pink wallpaper and a pink flamingo border running around the top of the room. The demarcation line between the family room and the kitchen consisted of white-filigreed gingerbread latticework attached to the ceiling in the breakfast nook part of the family room.

The kitchen had original white painted cabinets, dated appliances, a white tile floor, and a white plastic laminate countertop that showed stains easily. There was pastel wallpaper throughout the kitchen, including three layers of wallpaper on the ceiling. Before long, the homeowners started calling their renovation project *No More Pink Flamingos*.

In addition to updating the look, the couple wanted to improve the functionality of the kitchen. There was much unused space that they wanted to convert into usable storage. In addition, they wanted to raise the counters to a more comfortable working height.

After some research, the couple selected stock cabinets with clean designs, and features they were unable to find elsewhere. They also learned a leading consumer research magazine gave their supplier a top rating for quality.

These homeowners dramatically transformed a pink flamingo–themed kitchen with warm cherry cabinets and stylish accents.

THE GOALS

① **Maximize Storage Space:** Replace soffits with cabinetry and add pullouts for easy accessibility.

② **Update the Look:** Use warm wood tones, high-end appliances, and stylish accents to give this 1980 era kitchen a fresh and modern makeover.

THE PLAN

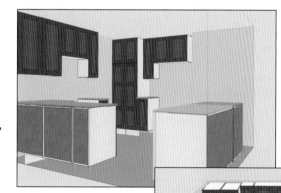

The homeowner, using downloadable software created this 3-D view of the proposed kitchen.

After drawing the original plan on the computer, it is easy to switch to a different angle such as this elevated view.

① MAXIMIZE STORAGE SPACE

There was a lot of wasted space in the old kitchen. The soffits above all of the top cabinets consumed valuable wall space without serving a purpose. Additionally, the lower cabinets, which all had one drawer and a large door without any pullouts, were not working to their full potential. Because the homeowners are tall (6'0" and 6'5"), it was difficult for them to keep things easily accessible and organized in the bottom of the lower cabinets. New ceiling-height upper cabinets and lower cabinets with pullout drawers have dramatically improved the storage issue.

All of the lower cabinets in the new kitchen are now deep drawers, pullouts, or lazy Susans.

REMOVE SOFFITS

Additional vertical storage space was gained in the new kitchen by removing the existing soffits and replacing them with ceiling height cabinets.

CREATE A CUSTOM LOOK

The original pantry featured a standard folding door that did not help the look of the new kitchen. To create visual continuity between it and the rest of the room, Greg and Mary Kate replaced the folding door with doors made from upper cabinet doors. The installer made the new pantry doors by stacking one door on the other and attaching them to thick plywood backing. This gives the pantry doors a custom look without the custom price. With the new cabinet space available in the rest of the kitchen, the formerly overstuffed pantry now finds a new use as storage for small appliances.

New matching doors on the existing pantry create a cohesive look throughout the kitchen.

Upper cabinet doors are joined together and attached to plywood to create a custom look on this foldout door.

② UPDATE THE LOOK

The old pink and white design scheme just did not work for Greg and Mary Kate. They wanted a kitchen that not only functioned well, but one that better reflected their personalities. Mary Kate is fun loving and artistic. She selected the iridescent blue tiles to add some pizzazz to the room. Greg loves the outdoors and is a creative cook. He loves the warm wood tones of the cabinets and newly installed hardwood floors.

This stylish kitchen makeover included all new appliances, cabinets, countertops, and flooring.

APPLIANCES

The appliances in the existing kitchen were tired and dated. For the new kitchen, the homeowners replaced the old stove, microwave, and refrigerator with contemporary black appliances. The combination of the black appliances with silver handles and the natural cherry cabinets create a beautiful look for this kitchen. The refrigerator is a side-by-side French door-style with the freezer below. By shopping carefully, the homeowners saved $900 on this highly rated refrigerator.

The homeowners felt their new side-by-side door refrigerator was their "one big splurge" on this project.

The new black appliances complement the natural cherry cabinets.

NEW FLOOR

The existing kitchen had a cold and outdated white porcelain tile floor that extended to the family room, foyer, and solarium. To install a new floor, the couple first had to tear out the 800 square feet of tile. (It took the homeowners six days to chip-hammer it all away!) They replaced the tile in all of the rooms with beautiful Brazilian cherry hardwood. Because their house is built on a slab, the homeowners wisely had a plumber come out and video snake the kitchen sink pipes to ensure there were no obstructions or problems *before* putting down the hardwood floor.

This gorgeous Brazilian cherry floor replaced 800 square feet of cold white tile.

An iridescent inkwell glass-tile backsplash above the countertop and appliances add a unique touch.

STYLISH ACCENTS

The kitchen needed some unique design features that would allow the homeowners to put their personal touch on the projects.

Counters

The original white laminate countertop was outdated and stained easily. To update the look, all new countertops made of Silestone® were installed. Silestone is an engineered stone made primarily of quartz. It comes in 65 unique colors, is highly scratch and stain resistant, and does not need to be sealed. It costs about $30 less per square foot than granite.

The original counters were not only outdated, but they were too low. To create a more comfortable workspace, Greg and Mary Kate raised the counters, but not so high that it will jeopardize resale of the home in the future.

Blue glass knobs on the upper cabinets add color and beauty to this kitchen without adding a lot of extra cost.

Instead of traditional toe kick plates, the homeowners used contemporary steel legs that match the handles on the refrigerator and lower cabinets.

Sleek white Silestone replaces the white laminate countertops that stained easily.

THE AFTER

Greg and Mary Kate are very pleased with the new look of their kitchen, and immediately felt comfortable working in it because they kept the appliances and sink in the same positions. They are currently expecting a child and are thrilled that the new kitchen has plenty of room to store baby food and other necessities.

To save money, they did a lot of research and whatever work they were comfortable with themselves. For example, they painted the walls and did the tedious jobs, such as wallpaper removal, but hired professionals to do some of the finishing work. They also recycled old materials whenever possible. Their old cabinets were snapped up on *www.freecycle.org*, which meant they were recycled and did not have to hire someone to haul them away.

They also were not afraid to purchase online. In addition to the refrigerator and other items, they found the tile for the backsplash for under $10 per square foot. Friends purchased the same backsplash locally for closer to $20 per square foot.

One mistake they believe they made was to have an electrician install dimmers, light switches, and outlets. A professional was costly and, in retrospect, they believe that with some research, they could have installed them themselves. (**Author's Note:** If you have any doubts about your ability to do electrical work, hire a licensed electrician.) They also did not have canned lighting installed and wish they had. They plan to add it soon.

What about the wooden floors in the kitchen? Despite the concrete slab foundation, the wooden floors have not been a problem. Because they were properly finished, they have remained perfectly flat and are easy to clean.

Overall, the *No More Pink Flamingos* project was a beautiful, practical, *and* affordable success!

CHAPTER 3

Lessons in Design

If you are reading this book, then you may be frustrated with your old kitchen and ready to tear it out immediately. That is okay, but before doing so, take some time to plan and design your new kitchen. I recommend starting the process by making a list of what, if anything, you like about your old kitchen and what you dislike about it as well. Going through that process will help you create a new kitchen design based on your needs and help you avoid what you did not like about your old kitchen.

I recently tore out and completely rebuilt the kitchen in our house using affordable stock cabinets. You will see many photos of it in various stages of completion in this book. Carpenters built the original kitchen on-site in 1968 and more than 40 years later, it was literally falling apart (**Figure 3-1**). The overall layout seemed haphazard and there was a lot of wasted space. The original wasted space was a good thing when it came to remodeling because there was indeed quite a bit of space to work with. Removing the overhanging soffits from above the cabinets opened up even more space.

A wall with a pass-through opening separated the original kitchen from the dining area. I removed the wall to create even more space and give the room more of an open feeling.

[SPECIAL TERM]
Soffit: *The boxed-in area between the top of the upper (wall) cabinets and the ceiling. Soffits are sometimes called bulkheads and are common in older homes.*

Figure 3-1. Squeezed into a corner, the refrigerator was inconvenient to access. Note the haphazard storage without any doors or drawers.

Figure 3-2. The new kitchen is much improved with ample stock cabinetry and a better layout.

LIKES AND DISLIKES

We started our project by sitting down and writing out what we liked and disliked about the old kitchen. Some of the things you may want to include on your list are the layout, storage, cabinet style and color, hardware, and countertops. Also consider eating and food preparation areas, position of windows, doors, walls, sinks, and types of appliances, flooring, electrical, and lighting. Here are our lists:

Likes:

Jon's Likes:
- Large space
- Two relatively large windows with good views
- Sink under window
- One long counter

Sherry's Likes:
- Radiant heat in the floor

Dislikes:

Jon's Dislikes:
- Refrigerator inaccessible in corner
- Dishwasher inaccessible in corner and blocks adjacent cabinets
- Wasted space because two walls have no counters or cabinets
- Wasted space in corner cabinets
- Wall for pass-through seems unnecessary
- Countertops are falling apart and require constant maintenance

Sherry's Dislikes:
- Too little storage
- Poor shelving in upper cabinets
- Dead space in corners
- Cannot open dishwasher unless adjacent cabinets are all the way closed or open
- Cabinets falling apart
- Cheap faucet
- Shallow sink
- Not enough drawers
- No outside entry
- Refrigerator against wall so freezer door will not open all the way
- Uneven counters (caused by settling)
- Cheap stove
- Windows hard to open
- Exhaust fan not vented outside
- No work triangle
- Dead, inefficient space in middle of room
- Doorway against wall coupled with refrigerator location makes one wall useless
- Inadequate lighting

BUDGET

One of the primary considerations when designing any kitchen is the budget. A kitchen is one of the costliest parts of any house, and final cost can vary tremendously. I have worked on residential kitchens with budgets of more than $100,000.

This book features the kitchen I built for my own home. The project cost slightly more than $12,000 (detailed below) using stock cabinets, mid-level stainless steel appliances, and 2' by 2' (610mm by 610mm) granite tile for the countertops. Of course, this did not include any labor because I did all of the work myself (except for one helper for a couple of days). Here were the actual costs for my kitchen:

Benson's Kitchen Costs	
Appliances*	$4,517
Cabinets (includes crown molding)	$4,964
Countertops (includes backsplash tile, tile board, cement and grout)	$1,079
Floor	$600
Sink	$200
Faucet	$135
Lighting	$350
Door Handles and Drawer Pulls	$150
Drywall, Drywall Compound, Paint	$130
Tool Rental (drywall lift and tile saw)	$125
Trash Removal	$60
Total	$12,310

*One way to lower the cost would be to buy less expensive appliances.

[SPECIAL TERM]
HVAC: *A specialist in heating, ventilation, and air conditioning.*

The budget for a kitchen will have a great impact on all aspects of any kitchen design. The most expensive category in many kitchens (other than labor) is the cabinets. The fact that I used stock cabinets from a home improvement store definitely lowered the cost (more information on *stock cabinets* in Chapter 4). Cabinets typically are more than 50% of the total cost, but were only 37% of the total cost in our kitchen.

The cabinets probably have the most profound effect on the appearance and function of a kitchen but the countertops and appliances are next. A breakdown of each of these areas will help you to get a handle on your budget. Most people will emphasize one or two of these areas and then cut back on the others depending on their needs. For example, someone who cooks a lot may spend more on appliances and have more storage and cabinets, but in a lower price range. If you like to entertain in your kitchen, you may want to spend more on the cabinets and countertops and less on appliances.

Another cost to consider is the relocation of plumbing and wiring. Keeping the sink in the same general area will help keep costs down. The cost of moving or adding a sink to another area of the kitchen includes adding new drain pipe, possibly a new vent pipe through the ceiling and roof, and running new supply lines for the hot and cold water. A sink usually can be moved from a few inches up to a foot or two without much added expense just by extending the existing pipes. One thing that does not add much cost is adding or running a cold water supply line for an icemaker. (Even if it involves a considerable distance.)

Moving electrical wiring can vary in expense and in most cases more will need to be added to fit the needs of a modern kitchen and pass any state or local building codes. It may be very expensive to move any heating and cooling vents or pipes. If you cannot work around the existing vents and pipes, consult an HVAC professional or a plumber to create a plan.

Perhaps the most important decision in preparing a budget is whether you are going to:

- do all of the work yourself (as described in this book);

- be your own general contractor and do some of the work yourself and hire out individual subcontractors (plumbing, heating, drywall, electrical, flooring, etc.); or

- hire a general licensed contractor to manage the whole project.

A general contractor takes responsibility for hiring subcontractors, driving the schedule, and dealing with the headaches. A general contractor will usually earn about 15% to 20% of the whole cost. To that you have to add the labor of the subcontractors. The subcontractors can have more than 50% of their total costs in labor. This can vary tremendously depending on the trade, however. For example, cabinet installers will install a lot of dollars worth of cabinets in a set period of time whereas a plumber or electrician will spend a lot of time using much less materials. (Note: Another cost is a kitchen designer, if you do not do this yourself. In many cases if you hire a general contractor, he/she will also do the design work.)

Over the years, I have learned some important lessons in budgets and kitchen design ideas. Here is a summary of my *14 Ways to Save Money* as you plan your remodeled kitchen:

14 WAYS TO SAVE MONEY

1. Pre-plan so standard-sized, pre-made cabinets will fit into openings.
2. Buy stock cabinets from a home improvement center.
3. Install the cabinets yourself.
4. Do not move heating, air conditioning, ventilation, electrical, and plumbing (unless you absolutely have to).
5. Do not tear out load-bearing walls, windows, or doors.
6. Do not buy top-of-the-line appliances (unless you are really into cooking or they are on sale).
7. Do not use solid granite, custom-sized countertops. (Consider granite tiles.)
8. Do not use solid hardwood flooring. (Consider laminate flooring.)
9. Buy unfinished cabinets and finish them yourself.
10. Do not add an abundance of glass cabinet doors.
11. Do not buy expensive hardware. (When buying hardware ask for *contractor's pricing* such as *contractor's 10 packs*.)
12. Have your plumber or electrician stop at the *stub in* phase and install the fixtures yourself.
13. Make your own specialty storage organizers (i.e. utensil dividers, waste bins, pot and pan dividers, spice racks, etc.).
14. Attend a seminar at your local home improvement store to learn a new technique.

[SPECIAL TERM]

Load-bearing wall:
An interior wall that supports the weight of an upper floor and/or roof. Rafters, joists, or supports usually run perpendicular to a load-bearing wall and rest on it. Removing it usually requires additional reinforcement such as a large header or beam. Consult an architect or licensed contractor before removing a load-bearing wall.

WORK TRIANGLE

Once you have considered your budget and the impact various aspects of it will have on your finished kitchen, you can begin seriously thinking about laying out your new kitchen. The layout of most any kitchen starts with the *work triangle*. It is the most basic element of kitchen design and descended from professional kitchen practices.

The work triangle stresses three work areas or appliances (sink, stove, and refrigerator) are arranged in a triangle so the cook can either be facing one and reach from side to side to reach the other two or the cook can turn one way to reach the other two. The three stations should be in close proximity to each other. An ideal kitchen would have each side of the triangle between 4' (1.2m) and 9' (2.7m) apart (from center to center):

- Sink to Refrigerator = 4' to 7' (1.2m to 2.1m)
- Refrigerator to Stove = 4' to 9' (1.2m to 2.7m)
- Stove to Sink = 4' to 6' (1.2m to 1.8m)

> **QUICK TIP**
>
> The island can also become part of the work triangle, which can help the kitchen become more efficient. However, they also can break up the flow of the work triangle. If possible, keep islands, peninsulas, cabinets, and dining tables out of the basic triangle.

Figure 3-3. This kitchen has a long island with a sink. Notice the way the sink is set down lower behind a ledge to hide dirty dishes.

These figures allow a minimum of 12' (3.7m) of counter space and a maximum of 22' (6.7m). Too little counter space between these areas will not allow you to space work or handle food safely and too much distance means you will be spending your time inefficiently walking back and forth between the three stations rather than preparing food. If there are two (or more) people working in the kitchen at the same time, allow more than the usual 4-foot minimum between work centers.

A cook top on an island can greatly improve the efficiency of the work triangle. A sink can too, but it is a good idea to have a ledge on the island to hide dirty dishes (**Figure 3-3**).

The work triangle rule also can apply to smaller areas in the kitchen. For example, the vegetable cutting area can be within a triangle with the sink and the refrigerator. In addition, the vegetable cutting knives can be stored in a smaller triangle with the cutting area and trash or garbage disposal. This is a good thought process to get into when making many of the decisions both large and small about where to place everything within the kitchen.

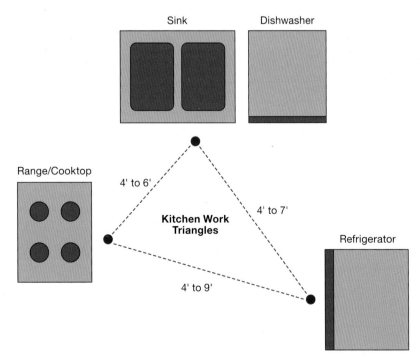

Figure 3-4. The work triangle in our new kitchen has the sink and dishwasher under the window, the stove to the right, refrigerator to the left, and lots of counter space in between.

Figure 3-5. The pullout compost container is conveniently located below the countertop where we cut vegetables.

Figure 3-6. With the stove located between the pans and lids in the lazy Susan on one side, and cutting knives on the other, it is convenient to cook and then slice meat hot from the oven.

Figure 3-7. Keeping the spices and oils just above the stove means we do not have to take any extra steps when working on the cook top on the range.

Our newly remodeled kitchen (**Figure 3-4**) has a work triangle layout for the major appliances, and the area around each appliance has the necessary items within easy reach. The vegetable cutting area is between the sink and the refrigerator, with the cutting boards and trash on one side and the vegetable knives and a compost box on the other (**Figure 3-5**). The stove has the pans, lids, and hot pads stored on one side and meat cutting knives and sheet pans and utensils on the other side (**Figure 3-6**). The cooking oils and spices are just above the stove for easy reach as well (**Figure 3-7**).

If you really want to save steps, keep your glassware, dishes, china, and plastic storage containers close to the sink and dishwasher (**Figures 3-8** to **3-10**). You will no doubt have other configurations and additional stations to set up, but the work triangle is a good place to start.

Figure 3-8. Placing a wall cabinet near the sink and dishwasher makes it easy to grab a glass for a drink of water and unload clean glasses into the cabinet.

Figure 3-9. The most convenient place to store dishes and plates is in the wall cabinet right near the dishwasher.

Figure 3-10. A lazy Susan is a great place to keep plastic storage containers. Placing it next to the dishwasher adds to the convenience.

QUICK TIP

As you lay out your work triangles keep in mind that work usually is done in one direction around the triangle. That is, when it is being prepared, food moves from the refrigerator to the mixing center or sink and then to the stove. After rinsing at the sink, the dishes move into the dishwasher and then up into the cabinets. If the main cook in your family is right handed or left handed, it might be most efficient to lay out the triangles so the majority of the work will move clockwise or counterclockwise around the triangles.

MORE QUICK RULES

Here are some more quick rules:

1. Keep the dishwasher within 36" (914mm) of the sink. Not only does this make it easier to rinse dishes before placing in the dishwasher, but also it is easier to make short plumbing hookups between the dishwasher and the sink.

2. Always have counter space next to the refrigerator to set items as they are removed from the refrigerator or freezer. There should be a minimum of 15" (381mm) of counter space on the latch side of the refrigerator. If it is a side-by-side refrigerator, allow for 15" (381mm) on each side.

KITCHEN LAYOUT

With an understanding of the basic work triangle, now it is time to get serious about laying out the kitchen. There are a number of ways to get your ideas onto paper and to the layout stage. Several computer programs are available specifically for designing kitchens. 20-20 Design (*www.2020technologies.com*), designed especially for kitchen design professionals, allows you to draw not only floor plans but also 3-D photo-realistic renderings. SmartDraw (*www.Smartdraw.com*) offers free downloadable trial software that would be a good choice if you are only designing one kitchen. It starts with existing kitchen design templates. From there you can change the size of the kitchen to match yours

and add appliances and cabinets. The result is a floor plan you can work with or take to a kitchen design consultant or contractor.

Some home improvement stores and cabinet manufacturers have online kitchen design pages on their websites that allow you to design your kitchen, add the appliances, see it all in three dimensions, and print it out. You can view the kitchen with the various cabinets the store carries, and then order the cabinets online for pick up at the store or for delivery to your house. I have found this to be a great way to draw up ideas and then get the exact cabinets I want delivered. Your drawing can be stored for use as you work and opened at the store by the sales staff if they have questions.

[SPECIAL TERM]

Architect's ruler: *A special triangular-shaped ruler that has six scales (for example 1 inch = 1 foot; ¼" = 1'; or 1½" = 1').*

QUICK TIP

If you use a professional design consultant, ask to see drawings and photos (if available) of other kitchens they have designed. Ask for references you can call and maybe even visit.

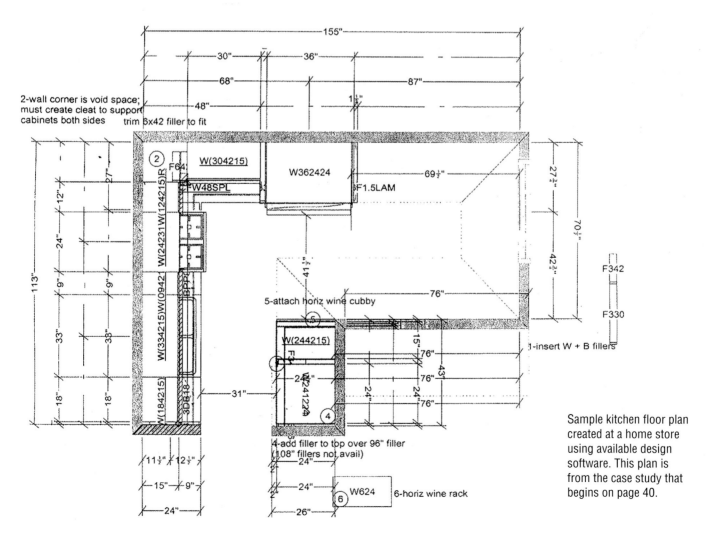

Sample kitchen floor plan created at a home store using available design software. This plan is from the case study that begins on page 40.

If your local store does not provide this service online, you can visit the store and the sales staff should be able to help you create a design using one of the software programs mentioned above or another program they use with customers.

As you begin to design out your new kitchen, review your priorities (Introduction) and the things you did or did not like about your old kitchen (page 61). Keep these ideas in mind throughout the whole design process.

A good way to get started looking at options and where to place everything so it will all fit is to draw out a scaled drawing on graph paper. Make each square a set distance (i.e. one inch equals one foot) and consider using an architect's ruler. Then you can quickly add in and take out items without a lot of measuring. Transparent tracing paper placed over earlier drafts drawn on the graph paper will also help to speed things up. It will probably take a few, if not many versions, to get the design you like and still have everything fit into the space and within your budget.

Once you have a drawing or two down on paper and have torn out the existing cabinets (see Chapter 5), you can apply tape to the floor and walls to get a better idea how it will feel in your actual kitchen (**Figure 3-11**). I applied tape to the floor of our kitchen and determined there was not enough room for an island, so we decided to remove a wall and create a peninsula that would give us an eat-in kitchen.

STARTING YOUR DRAWING

Start by placing the items into your drawing that you do not want to move or cannot easily move. I call these *fixed points*. They include the ends of the room, windows, exterior doors, load-bearing walls, vent hood pipes that go through the ceiling, and appliances with limited options for moving. After these are on the drawing, place in any corner cabinets or lazy Susans as they are fixed points as well.

Note: It is a good idea to have the *exact* dimensions of your appliances before ordering the cabinets as appliance sizes can vary. Most

QUICK TIP

Once you have your appliance dimensions, use your architect's ruler to lay out and then cut miniature appliances to perfect scale out of poster board. You can easily move these around on your drawing to determine their best position.

Figure 3-11. By applying masking tape to the floor, you can quickly get a sense if there will be enough room for the cabinets and appliances you want.

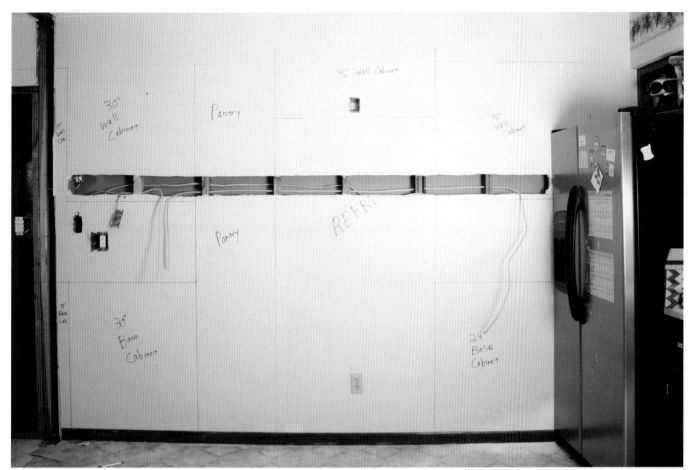

Figure 3-12. With the old cabinets torn out, you can mark the location and size of the new cabinets right on the walls.

dishwashers are the same size. Ranges (a cook top and oven combination) come in just a few standard sizes. The sizes of stand-alone ovens, cook tops, and refrigerators can vary tremendously so pay particular attention to these dimensions before committing to any particular size of cabinets.

Stock cabinets come in standard sizes. (For more about standard cabinet dimensions, see Chapter 4.) Use these standards to plug them in between the fixed points. Altering these cabinets is possible if you have a little woodworking experience, although minimizing alterations serves the project best. (For more about altering a cabinet, see pages 119-123.) It is usually much easier to add spacers between two cabinets or make a spacer to fit into the space along the wall at the end of a row of cabinets than it is to alter the size of a cabinet.

Once the drawings are complete, you can lay out the design directly on the walls for use as a reference for plumbing, wiring, plastering, and painting (**Figure 3-12**). You do not need to finish and paint the area behind the cabinets, although building codes will most likely require you to cover any holes in the drywall to prevent the spread of fire.

DESIGN VS. PLUMBING

Many kitchens will have the sink centered on a window and then the rest of the cabinets will radiate out from there. If your existing plumbing will allow it, it makes sense to start the design of that wall from there. In our old kitchen, the sink centered on a window, which meant the dishwasher had to be forced up against the side of the adjacent cabinet (**Figure 3-13**). In some cases, using a smaller sink or moving the dishwasher will help to keep the sink centered while making other changes. In this case, there just was not enough room to fit everything in, keep it visually centered, and still have a dishwasher that would open easily while allowing the nearby cabinets to open as well.

The solution here was to make everything look as centered as possible without actually centering the sink or the lower cabinets. What really makes this work is the fact that everything from the countertop up is centered on the window, including the faucet (**Figure 3-14**).

I was able to find a sink that fit into the space with a faucet hole that could be centered on the window. I then installed a large faucet that raises up high enough to divert attention away from the sink itself. The upper cabinets then were centered out from the window. The only added spacing in the entire kitchen was a 1½" (38mm) spacer in the upper-right side (**Figure 3-15**).

For the lower cabinets, I started with the two lazy Susan units in the corners and then worked in toward the center. The lower cabinets could not be centered on the window either, but the centered upper cabinets, the faucet, and the light fixture help to create the illusion that everything is centered. To me, having an accessible dishwasher and a lazy Susan in each corner far outweighed this visual aspect of the design.

Figure 3-13. In our original kitchen, it was a tight fit with the dishwasher door opening up tight against the adjacent cabinets.

Figure 3-14. Note in the finished kitchen that the upper cabinets, faucet, and light fixture center on the window even though the sink is offset to the left to allow clearance on the right side of the dishwasher.

Figure 3-15. To keep everything as visually centered as possible, I added a 1½" spacer between two cabinets. Later I finished it to match the other cabinets. (For more on the process of adding a spacer, see Chapter 6.)

RESTAURANT LESSONS FROM A PRO
Work Flow

The type and volume of food the restaurant serves largely determines the design of a professional kitchen. A barbeque restaurant kitchen will have a much different design than a Chinese restaurant. A fast food kitchen is completely different from a kitchen producing haute cuisine.

Because efficiency is so important in the design of a professional kitchen, certain areas of the kitchen may be designed for specific purposes. Areas may include:

- Salad preparation
- Grilling
- Deep frying
- Desserts
- General meal preparation
- Clean-up

Busy restaurants will have cooks assigned to specific areas during rush periods. A sous chef, for example, will stand in front of the griddle with the correctly portioned out food to be cooked close at hand in some type of refrigerated cooler. The pans for cooking and clean plates for serving will also be within easy reach.

This diner has everything needed for egg and omelet preparation set up right near the front of the house for quick access. (Note: The *front of the house* refers to the area where the customers eat and the *back of the house* refers to the kitchen.)

The home cook must be a Jack (or Jill) of all trades, and have a kitchen that can accommodate that fact. However, each home kitchen can have task areas that allow the flow of the kitchen to be as smooth as possible. For example, proper placement of the major appliances in relation to each other and to the sink (i.e. the work triangle) can minimize the effort it takes to remove food from the refrigerator, clean it in the sink, and cook and serve it.

UNIVERSAL DESIGN

You may have heard of the concept of *universal design*, a phrase that first became popular in the 1970s. When most people hear the phrase, they think of special changes made in a layout or home plan especially for the disabled. However, the important term is *universal*. The idea is to make a home more easily usable for people of all ages, sizes, and abilities, whether disabled or not. Wider doorways with lever set hardware and additional task or stairway lighting would be examples of universal design. Not only do these provide easier use, but a margin of safety for everyone.

The special challenge here is to make the look of a universally designed home (and here, the kitchen) as unobtrusive or even invisible as possible. This will help prevent stigmatizing or segregating some users. Some of the principles of universal design are to make different processes around the house easy to understand, regardless of a user's experience, and to allow the user to work with a minimum of fatigue and physical effort. If possible, all components and hardware (faucets, handles, etc.) should be as comfortable to reach whether standing or sitting.

Many of these features can be added to an existing kitchen, but it is most cost effective to do it when you are first building or totally remodeling a kitchen. So when laying out your kitchen, take into consideration the needs you not only have now, but the needs you may have in the future.

Some of the specific things you can do in a kitchen include:

- Build countertops at varying heights for different tasks. For an average-sized person, the working surface should be 28" to 36" (711mm to 914mm) high and the usable counter space is 16" (406mm) wide.

- Use pullout work surfaces such as breadboards and cutting boards for easy access when sitting in a chair.

- Lower the upper (wall) cabinets so they are closer to the lower (base) cabinets.

- Add D-shaped, loop handles on cabinet doors and drawers.

- Use full-extension drawer guides that make it easier to access everything in the drawer (see Chapter 4).

- Install pullout shelves, lazy Susans, and special organizing hardware (see Chapter 4).

- Install a sink with a shallow (5" to 6" [127mm to 152mm] deep) basin.

- Install a *faux* cabinet door under the sink or eliminate the door completely so the sink is wheelchair accessible. By using a tub-bend pipe, move the drain back to provide knee room. Insulate hot water pipes under the sink.

- Use a loop-handled kitchen faucet with push-button sprayer controls.

- Select a side-by-side refrigerator so the freezer is easily accessible.

- Shop for a cook top or range with controls on or near the front.

- Install the dishwasher at least 6" to 8" (152mm to 203mm) above the floor and accessible from the right or left hand side.

- Use non-slip flooring or low-pile carpeting.

- When deciding where to place islands, peninsulas, and tables, be aware it takes an area of five feet square of open area for a wheelchair user to make a 360° turnaround.

- All access doors should be a minimum of 32" (813mm) wide (36" [914mm] is preferred).

- Mount switches and thermostats 48" (1,219mm) above the floor and electrical outlets no lower than 15" (381mm) above the floor.

CHAPTER 4

All About Cabinets

(What to Know Before You Go Shopping)

The cabinets are the real heart of any kitchen-remodeling job. They probably have the greatest impact on the overall appearance of the kitchen, and can be the largest single expense. Understanding cabinet styles and construction before going shopping or talking to a kitchen designer about your new kitchen plans is worthwhile.

THREE CATEGORIES OF CABINETS

There are three general categories of kitchen cabinets: custom, semi-custom, and stock. There are different varieties of each.

Custom cabinets are the most expensive type of cabinets. A cabinet shop makes custom cabinets for a specific kitchen from a plan designed by an architect or a kitchen designer. The maker of the custom cabinets usually installs and configures them to create an almost unlimited variety of storage and organizational solutions from any wood or color combination and in almost any set of dimensions or style.

Their versatility comes at a cost, however, because they are the most expensive type of cabinets. I have seen the custom cabinets for an elaborate kitchen run as high as $60,000. A common figure might be $500 to $850 per running foot but can go as high as $1,000. (Note: The price includes lazy Susans and pullouts.) A running foot refers to one foot in width that includes *both* the upper and the lower cabinets. Most custom kitchens end up in the $750 to $850 range. This includes the cabinets, installation, and handles only. It does not include the countertops, plywood to support the countertops, plumbing, wiring, flooring, or anything else.

Probably the most commonly installed cabinets by contractors are *semi-custom cabinets.* Home improvement stores, kitchen designers,

or contractors order semi-custom cabinets from the manufacturer. The majority of semi-custom cabinets are ordered in stock sizes then a few of the cabinets are custom-sized to fit into a particular space or to fill a specific need. Manufacturers can custom size the cabinets or they can be altered after delivery.

Semi-custom cabinets are available in many styles, woods, and colors. They often average about $500 per running foot (installed), but cost can vary tremendously. Outlets that sell these cabinets will often have a connection to contractors who can install the cabinets as well as any necessary plumbing and electrical work.

The cabinets shown in this book and the ones I used in our kitchen remodel are *stock cabinets.* They are the most inexpensive way to get a new kitchen in your home. I paid about $160 per running foot for the stock cabinets (not including installation). They are cabinets that are in stock at most home improvement stores and some lumber yards. They come in a limited variety of colors and sizes. However, as you will see in this book, with a little additional work and some classic-looking hardware, you can make these cabinets look great in your kitchen. In fact, once the kitchen is completed it is difficult to tell from outward appearances if the project used custom, semi-custom, or stock cabinets.

MATERIALS

Cabinets are made from a variety of wood species and materials. These can vary by the look you want and your budget. They also can vary in appearance based on the hundreds of stains, glazes, and paints applied. Here are some of the most common materials used to build kitchen cabinets:

WOOD SPECIES
(listed from least to most expensive)

Oak (plainsawn). Plainsawn oak has a strong open grain pattern that varies from closely knit to sweeping arch patterns. Its natural color can range from white to yellow to reddish brown.

Maple. Maple is a strong wood that is usually off-white in color. It is uniform in appearance, making it ideal for a clean look. It is often straight-grained but can be wavy or curly.

Birch. Natural birch is a medium-dense wood with a distinctive grain pattern. The predominant color is white to creamy yellow, but the heartwood can be dark brown or even reddish brown.

Hickory. Hickory is a strong open-grained wood with a flowing grain pattern and dramatic variations in color. Hickory often contains mineral streaks and might vary from light to deep brown in color, making each hickory kitchen unique.

Oak (quartersawn). Quartersawn oak is cut across the growth rings and its grain pattern is more subtle and straight than plainsawn oak. Quartersawn has a more traditional look.

Cherry. Cherry is a very rich, multi-colored hardwood, often used in fine furniture. It has pinkish-brown hues with shades of white or gray. It may contain small pitch pockets and pin knots. It will naturally darken as it ages.

CASE MATERIALS

• Solid veneer plywood (best)

• Solid veneer-covered particleboard or medium density fiberboard (MDF) (second best)

• Paper, melamine, or thermo foil-covered plywood or MDF (lowest quality)

• Solid wood (Rarely used in the actual cases. Used for face frames, doors, drawers, and occasionally shelves.)

DOOR AND DRAWER FRONT MATERIALS
(Should match wood species of face frames)

- Solid wood (best)
- Veneer plywood
- MDF (shaped and covered with veneer, plastic, or thermo foil)

[SPECIAL TERM]

MDF: *Medium-density fiberboard is a heavy, flat, and stable material made from fine wood fibers. It can be painted, covered with veneer or plastic laminate, or purchased with a thin-plastic covering called melamine already applied.*

DRAWER SIDE MATERIALS
(Does not have to match wood species of case materials)

- Solid wood (best)
- Veneer plywood (second best)
- Pre-fabricated metal or plastic
- Particleboard (lowest quality)

PRICING

If you are interested in semi-custom or stock cabinets, and are shopping at a home improvement store, they will often give you a quote for a 10' by 10' (3,048mm by 3,048mm) sample kitchen for simple comparison purposes. A 10' by 10' kitchen is actually two 10' (3,048mm) walls, not four. They include upper and lower cabinets and they usually count meeting corner units twice.

Unfinished stock oak cabinets run about $100 per running foot. The finished stock cabinets similar to what I used in our kitchen run about $150 to $170 per running foot. Our kitchen is 10' by 12' (3,048mm by 3,658mm), but it had three walls of cabinets for roughly 32 running feet. Since the cabinets cost about $5,000, I ended up paying about $160 per running foot. Special order cabinets from a home improvement store will run about $175 to $235 for a basic kitchen depending on the door style and finish.

A slightly higher-grade of cabinets (often called enhanced) can cost more than $300 per running foot. For that price, you get higher-end materials and finishes, more pullouts, storage organizers, and crown molding. Finally, they might have a high-end (fully equipped) line of cabinets with the highest quality woods, more millwork details, more pullouts, and storage organizers starting at around $500 per running foot (again, this is for the cabinets only—no installation).

Be aware, though, that buying cabinets is sort of like buying a new automobile. The actual price can vary tremendously based upon locality and how many options you want to add. In addition, the base price does not include molding, decorative hardware, special end panels, countertops, sinks, faucets, appliances, lighting, and other accessories.

Another issue is delivery. One of the home improvement chains ships six or less cabinets to your local store for you to pick up. If you order more than six cabinets, you can get them shipped directly to your home for a $150 delivery charge. Delivery will usually be within 2 to 3 weeks.

If you go online to the websites of most of the larger home improvement centers, you can select from a variety of colors and styles. One of them even offers to send you a sample cabinet door for $20. If you should purchase your cabinets from them, they will deduct the $20 from the price of your order. It is a good way to get the actual feel of the quality of the finish and workmanship, as well as how it would look in your kitchen.

FACE FRAME VS. FRAMELESS

In its simplest form, a cabinet is just a box. It usually has a back on it and sometimes a door on the front and drawers, which are themselves just boxes, inside.

Face frame cabinets have a frame over the front of the box. Because most cabinets are built of plywood, a solid wood face frame hides the plywood edging and provides an edge that can be fitted to the contours of an irregular wall (more on this in Chapter 6.) The face frame might be anywhere from 1" to 4" (25mm to 102mm) wide, with the most common being 1¾" (44mm) wide. Face frame cabinets are the most traditional and commonly available cabinets.

Frameless cabinets (known also as European-style cabinets) do not have a frame. Instead, thin bands of wood or plastic cover the plywood's front edges. They have a sleeker look and it is possible to have a clean, flat plane of just doors and drawers. However, they do require special hinges. Frameless cabinets have become increasingly popular in the United States for contemporary style kitchens.

Face Frame vs. Frameless Cabinet

WHAT TO LOOK FOR IN CABINETS

Everybody loves a bargain and I have pointed out above some of the real cost-saving advantages of using stock cabinets over custom cabinets. Generally, of course, the more you pay, the higher the quality. Sometimes, though, you can find stock cabinets with custom cabinet features.

Be a knowledgeable consumer. Open the doors and drawers and look inside. Ask questions of the salespeople or kitchen designer recommending a certain brand. If your budget allows it, you may want to step up to a higher quality stock cabinet or even a semi-custom cabinet. On the next couple of pages are some of the features you are likely to find in custom or semi-custom cabinets and would be a bonus if you found them in a stock cabinet.

QUICK TIP
Special-order cabinets often can include some of the features listed in the Kitchen Cabinet Quality Checklist on pages 80-81. A customer could install special-order cabinets and save a lot of money over custom cabinets. The major difference between custom-made and special-order cabinets is special-order cabinets are sold only in stock sizes. To change sizes and kitchen configurations, you have to order semi-custom or custom cabinets.

[SPECIAL TERM]

European-style cabinets: *After the destruction of World War II, the Europeans had to quickly rebuild their homes and a system of standardized kitchen cabinetmaking was developed. It is built on the idea of frameless cabinets and measurements with increments of 35mm.*

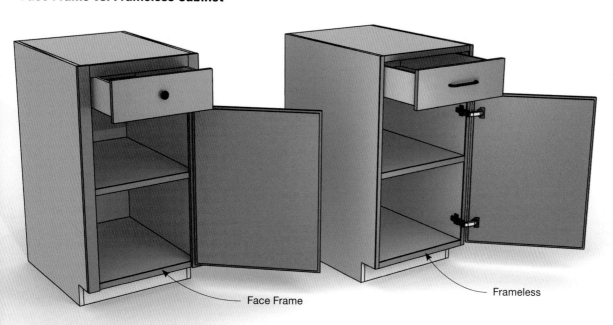

Face Frame

Frameless

Kitchen Cabinet Quality Checklist

☐ **Wood:** Are the cabinet face frames and doors built from a solid hardwood (such as cherry, walnut, oak, hickory, maple) or from a softer wood likely to get dents and dings (pine, poplar, some foreign woods)? Are the solid wood parts a full ¾" (19mm) or more thick?

☐ **Wood-engineered Materials:** Are the cabinet box sides, top, and bottom made from full ¾" (19mm)-thick materials (furniture-grade plywood or particleboard material)? Are the face layers (or plies) solid wood or just a wood design printed on paper? Is the back at least a full ¼" (6mm) thick?

☐ **Grain Pattern:** Are the face frames built from straight grain wood? (Note: Though swirly grain may be attractive, it is more likely to warp and cause problems. That is something you do not want in the face frames or door frames.) Are the grain patterns in other areas (doors and drawer fronts, cabinet sides) reasonably consistent? Here it is okay to have swirly grain as long as it does not get too wild looking when stained. Manufacturers save time and materials by just edge-gluing pieces of wood without considering their appearance. Look for grain patterns that seem to logically flow from one piece to the next.

☐ **Color Variations and Mineral Streaks:** Is the wood consistent in color on natural wood cabinets? Wood is a natural material and will change color over time. It also may contain dark mineral streaks. The best cabinet manufacturers will try to keep these to a minimum so as not to distract from the overall look of the kitchen. If possible, buy your cabinets all at the same time and from the same manufacturer so colors and grain patterns are consistent.

☐ **Joinery:** Though the type of joinery used is very important, it is one of the most difficult things to access because it is often hidden inside the wood. Are there lots of nails and staples? If you see them, that is generally not good. Manufacturers can save time and cut corners by simply air nailing or stapling two pieces of wood together instead of cutting quality interlocking joinery (such as mortise and tenons, tongue and grooves, or dadoes). Interlocking joints should be glued together for added strength, but dripping excess glue is a sign of sloppy craftsmanship.

☐ **Gussets:** Gussets are triangular-shaped blocks that reinforce corners usually at the top and sometimes at the bottom of a large base cabinet. They also can provide a place to screw up through to secure a countertop. Are they made from hardwood and both glued and screwed in place?

☐ **Hanging Rails:** Can the cabinets be well secured to the wall? This is especially important in hanging upper cabinets. Look inside the cabinets to see if they have a ¾" (19mm)-thick hanging rail near the top back of the cabinet. Some manufacturers leave this off and suggest you secure the cabinet simply with screws through the ¼" or ⅜" (6mm to 10mm)-thick back. That is not a very strong way to hold up a cabinet full of dishes, glasses, and/or food.

☐ **Shelves:** Are the shelves a full ¾" (19mm) thick and banded on the front edge so plywood layers or particleboard do not show? Is the banding solid wood that helps to prevent sagging and will not allow the veneer on the face of the shelf to chip off? Are the shelves adjustable with uniform rows of holes for shelf clips at the ends and in the middle for long shelves?

☐ **Drawers:** Pull open drawers and check the corner joints. Dovetail joints, for example, are some of the strongest drawer joints available (**Figure 4-1**). They will stand up to the constant opening and slamming of heavily loaded drawers. If the drawers are not dovetailed, they should be held together with some kind of an interlocking joint. A drawer assembled just with staples or nails will quickly come apart.

Also, notice the thickness of the sides and back of the drawer. Three-quarter-inch-thick solid wood sides and back are the best, though ½" (13mm) thickness is acceptable and by far the most common. The bottom should be a full ¼" (6mm) thick (usually plywood) or it will sag under weight. In addition, be sure sides fully capture the bottom and are not just nailed to it. The drawers do not have to be the same kind of wood as the rest of the cabinet. A light-colored hardwood such as maple or birch is fine.

Finally, check the quality of the drawer guides (also known as slides or runners). Are the guides attached to the sides or bottom corner of the drawer, or hidden under the drawer? There are three things to look for

Kitchen Cabinet Quality Checklist (continued)

Figure 4-1. Drawers with interlocking dovetail joints will usually outlast the cabinets.

Photo courtesy of Quality Custom Cabinets Inc.

Finish: If you are buying unfinished cabinets and plan to finish them yourself, check the quality of the final sanding. Look for deep scratches, especially across the grain that will become obvious when you stain and apply a clear topcoat.

They might be painted or stained and then coated with a clear topcoat of lacquer or a durable conversion varnish. There are a variety of finishes available and what may first look like defects may have been put there on purpose. If applied by hand, glazing may collect in corners and grooves to add soft highlights and shadows. Distressing adds artificial imperfections that imitate dents, wormholes, and natural wear signs that will make the cabinets similar in appearance to an antique.

It can be difficult to tell about the durability of a finish simply by looking at a sample in a store. Most cabinets today are finished with a number of coats of spray lacquer, lightly hand sanded between coats. Look for the depth of the finish and imagine how it might hold up, especially around wear points (door handles, drawer pulls, and near the floor where it is likely to get repeatedly rubbed against by shoes, kids, and pets).

here. First, of course, is how smoothly they operate. Some even are self-closing and gently pull the drawer closed as it is pushed in. Second, what is the maximum amount of weight they will support? Even though you will rarely fill a drawer to this weight, I recommend the guide be rated to hold a maximum of 70 pounds. Finally, check for the drawer guide's extension. Full or three-quarter extension are best because both allow you to easily reach what is in the back of the drawer. To check a drawer's extension, pull it out all the way and make sure only 4" (102mm) or less of the drawer hides in the cabinet. Also, check how easy it is to completely remove a drawer for cleaning or maintenance.

Door Hinges: Check the quality of the door hinges and if they are self-closing. The best hinges also hold the door open if the cabinets settle or are not leveled properly, and are securely mounted but still adjustable (**Figure 4-2**). That is, by simply loosening and retightening screws you can adjust the position of the door in up to six directions (left/right, up/down, in/out).

Figure 4-2. Modern hinges adjust to raise and lower the doors for easy alignment.

DOOR AND DRAWER STYLES

There are three main styles of door (and drawer fronts): Flush mount, full overlay, or half overlay. On a flush mount (sometimes referred to as *inset*) door, the door's face is flush with the frame. That is, the door fits *inside* the frame (**Figures 4-3** and **4-4**). It provides a clean, contemporary look but can be very hard to install to get a uniform gap all the way around the door. And it is even more difficult to keep the gap consistent as the doors, drawers, and cabinets settle.

On a full overlay door, the door is mounted so it completely overlaps the frame (**Figure 4-5**). Sometimes the overlap is large enough that it will even hide the frame of a face frame cabinet or the front edge of a frameless cabinet. Using full overlay doors can give a clean, modern look to a kitchen,

but the mass of a ¾" (19mm)-thick door sticking out beyond the frame can look a bit bulky.

The most widely used type of door, especially for face frame cabinets, is the half overlay door (**Figure 4-6**). It has a lip that runs all the way around the door. The lip serves two purposes. First, it makes the door look less bulky because it reveals only one-half or so of the door's thickness. Second, it is easier to mount because the lip hides any imperfections in the squareness of the door opening or the door itself that would cause uneven gaps.

Each of the door styles will require a slightly different kind of hinge. Some of the hinges are visible and some are hidden behind the door. So it is important to decide if you want the hinges to be shown throughout your kitchen or not.

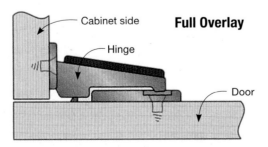

Figure 4-3. A flush-mounted door fits inside and is flush with the front of the face frame.

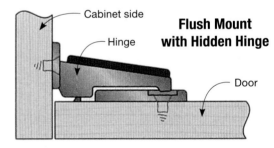

Figure 4-4. A flush-mounted door is sometimes called a *full recess* or *inset* door. This one features a European-style hinge that is hidden completely when the door is closed.

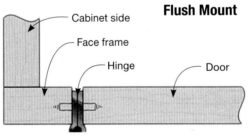

Figure 4-5. This full overlay door fits in front of the frameless cabinet and uses a European-style, highly adjustable hinge.

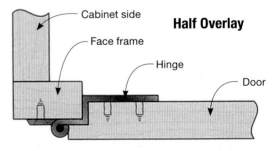

Figure 4-6. A half overlay door has a lip that hides any gap between the door and the face frame.

DOOR AND DRAWER FRONTS

One of the interesting (and fun) parts about selecting cabinets is you can dramatically change the appearance of your entire kitchen simply by changing the type of door and drawer front style you choose. The appearance of the door is determined as much by the construction technique as the desired look.

Made from a composite material (edge-banded plywood or MDF), flat-panel doors will not shrink or swell. They can be painted, stained, or covered with a veneer. Flat panel doors are usually flush mounted or used as full overlay doors (**Figure 4-7**).

Traditionally, cabinet doors and drawer fronts are constructed with a frame around the outside of a panel (**Figure 4-8**). Known as frame and panel construction, it is used in classic and country types of designs (**Figure 4-9**).

There is reason beyond the visual appearance for frame and panel design. If a door is solid wood in composition, it will expand and shrink with changes in humidity over the seasons. It would be difficult to keep all of the doors aligned and they

can warp as well. To counteract this, a wide solid wood panel is placed inside a slotted frame and allowed to float. It is not glued within the frame. The size of the frame and the overall door size remain the same and stay flat.

If the panel is solid wood, the edges can be shaped into a raised panel. A flat panel creates a more contemporary or Shaker appearance. A pane of glass as the panel allows you to display items within the cabinet. The panel also can be made of plywood or veneer-covered MDF.

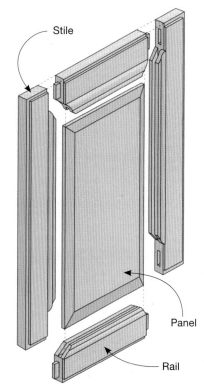

Figure 4-8. A solid wood raised panel housed within a frame keeps the panel from warping and still allows it to expand and contract.

Photo courtesy of Wood-Mode Fine Custom Cabinetry.

Photo courtesy of Crown Point Cabinetry.

Figure 4-7. Flat panel doors and drawer fronts create a clean, contemporary look to a kitchen.

Figure 4-9. Frame and panel construction can use a raised panel or flat panels as shown in this kitchen.

Refacing Cabinets

One alternative to completely remodeling a kitchen is to reface your cabinets. As long as you are happy with the current location and configuration of all of your cabinets, you can update and totally change the look of your kitchen and save thousands of dollars. Cabinet refacing requires no changes to your plumbing, electrical, ceilings, and floors. And, if you do not want to change the existing countertops, you can leave them in place.

You can do the work yourself or hire a contractor who specializes in cabinet refacing. There is a variety of door and drawer finishes and styles available. You start by choosing the door design, color, and finish and then measure the door and drawer front openings. Then measure the face frames and cabinet end panels. Installation involves cutting and fitting thin self-adhesive strips of wood veneer to the face frames or edges of frameless cabinets.

Another method is to paint the frames a matching or contrasting color to save even more money. After drying, the new doors and drawer fronts can be mounted and hung.

It is not a one-day project, but a handy person armed with a minimum amount of tools can do it easily.

Photo courtesy Quality Custom Cabinets Inc.

Before: A very typical bland kitchen from the 1950s–and a good candidate for cabinet refacing.

Photo courtesy Quality Custom Cabinets Inc.

After: By refacing the existing cabinets in natural maple and replacing the doors and drawer fronts, the kitchen stayed in the same configuration, but took on a modern appearance.

STANDARD CABINET DIMENSIONS

Most kitchen cabinets are sold in standardized dimensions designed for the average person (see information on special Universal Design in Chapter 3). For example, the distance from the floor to the top of the countertop is commonly 36" (914mm). A shorter cabinet may meet a special need, but also may make it difficult to sell the house later to someone of average height. It also may cause trouble when installing appliances such as a dishwasher that has to fit under a counter or a range you want to be level with the rest of the countertops.

Another example is the depth of the base cabinets. If they are too deep (front to back), the average person may not be able to reach over them to get into the upper wall cabinets. Or, if the upper wall cabinets are too small (front to back) they will not hold a standard 10" (254mm) dinner plate. Though they can be limiting, standard dimensions do make some sense. (And, remember, if you do have special requests, you can have your cabinets custom-made at an additional expense.)

Figure 4-10A shows the most common standard dimensions for kitchen cabinets.

Figure 4-10B details typical stock cabinet sizes.

Standard Kitchen Cabinets

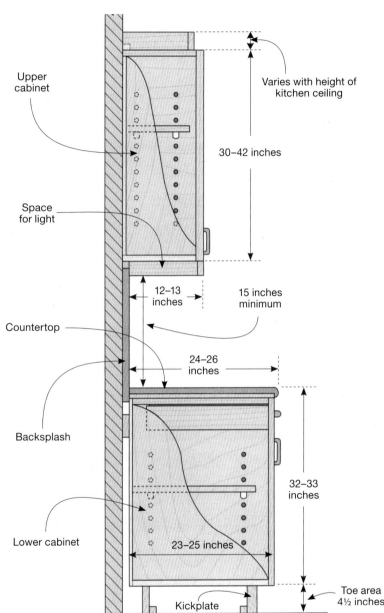

Figure 4-10A.

[SPECIAL TERM]

Toe area: *An area approximately 4" to 4½" (102mm to 114mm) high and set back about 3" (76mm) at the bottom of the base cabinets. It allows room for your feet to partially fit under the front of the cabinet so you can stand close. It can be created by setting the cabinet on top of a stand or as a notch cut out of the side of the cabinet. If it is a notch, it is covered with a kick plate strip. Cabinets can also sit on adjustable metal or plastic legs. (More about this in Chapter 6.)*

Stock Cabinet Sizes

	Height	Depth	Width
Lower (Base) Cabinets (includes toe area height, minus countertop)	34½" (876mm), 35" (889mm)	23¾" (603mm), 24" (610mm)	Drawer Cabinets: 18" (457mm), 24" (610mm) Single Door Cabinets (with one drawer above): 12" (305mm), 15" (381mm), 18" (457mm), 24" (610mm) Multiple Door Cabinets (with one drawer row above): 30" (762mm), 36" (914mm), 42" (1,067mm), 48" (1,219mm) Sink/Cook Top Cabinets: 30" (762mm), 32" (813mm), 36" (914mm), 42" (1,067mm), 48" (1,219mm)
Upper (Wall) Cabinets (includes face frame, but not the door)	30" (762mm), 36" (914mm), 42" (1,067mm)	12" (305mm)	Single Door: 12" (305mm), 15" (281mm), 18" (457mm), 24" (610mm) Double Door: 30" (762mm), 36" (914mm), 42" (1,067mm), 48" (1,219mm)
Wall Bridge Cabinets (to go over a stove, refrigerator, window, or sink)	12" (305mm), 15" (281mm), 18" (457mm)	12" (305mm)	30" (762mm), 36" (914mm), 39" (991mm), 48" (1,219mm)
Corner Upper (Wall) Cabinet	30" (762mm), 36" (914mm), 42" (1,067mm)	24" (610mm)	24" (610mm) with a 16" (406mm)-wide door
Corner Base Cabinet with Lazy Susan	34½" (876mm), 35" (889mm)	23¾" (603mm), 24" (610mm)	Installs in a 36" by 36" (914mm by 914mm) wall area
Oven Cabinets	84" (2,134mm), 90" (2,286mm)	24" (610mm)	33" (838mm)
Pantry Cabinets	84" (2,134mm), 90" (2,286mm)	24" (610 mm)	18" (457mm), 24" (610mm)

Figure 4-10B.

SPECIAL CABINETS

Corner cabinets can create special problems because of the wasted, inaccessible space behind where the two cabinets come together. This was the situation in my old kitchen (**Figure 4-11**).

There are two solutions to this problem. First, install a lazy Susan unit to provide easily accessible storage space (**Figures 4-12** and **4-13**). They are commonly 36" (914mm) across the front, leaving about 12" (305mm) exposed along each face.

Figure 4-11. The space in the corner inside the cabinets was inaccessible and wasted space. In addition, when the dishwasher door was opened, I could not open the cabinet door or drawer.

Figure 4-12. This lazy Susan is rated to hold up to 200 pounds (91kg) on two shelves. The doors are attached to the shelves and the entire unit rotates.

Figure 4-13. On this style of lazy Susan, a fixed door opens before the shelves rotate.

Figure 4-14. A corner wall cabinet extends out 12" (305mm) from the front face of the connecting cabinets. The door is 16" (406mm) wide.

A second solution is to use a corner cabinet with a diagonal front. This works best for an upper wall cabinet (**Figure 4-14**). It allows easy access to the space in the corner and takes up an area that is 24" by 24" (610mm by 610mm).

Other common types of cabinets are oven cabinets and pantry cabinets (**Figure 4-15**). These will usually be the same depth as the lower (base) cabinets, but the same height as the installed lower and upper cabinets combined (84" [2.1m] to 90" [2.3m]).

Figure 4-15. A pantry cabinet such as this one next to the refrigerator is handy for the storage of larger and taller items.

RESTAURANT LESSONS FROM A PRO

Mise en Place

Even during the peak rush hours, the restaurant kitchen can move food through quickly if everything has a place, is in its place, and can be easily accessed when needed. One of the classic principles of restaurant practice originated in France and is known as *mise en place*, or putting in its place. Having everything in its place first refers to having much of the food prepared ahead of time. Prep cooks will often come in to work before the serving time and prepare the food for cooking. Typical tasks would be cutting up vegetables, cutting and portioning out meats, pre-cooking or par boiling (partially cooking in water) certain parts of each dish and so on.

Everything is laid out ahead of time so chefs can easily grab what they need when cooking the food. As needed, they will bring in the extra bins of food in the rectangular pans prepared earlier.

The second part of *mise en place* is to have everything at hand when and where it is needed. Refrigerated storage units with standardized removable and replaceable trays or bins are stored right near the cook top. These trays or bins can be replaced quickly with ones that were pre-portioned and filled earlier and stored in larger walk-in or reach-in refrigerators farther away. The idea is to have as many of the most important items for a particular task nearby and have replacements and less important or less frequently used items farther and farther away. Having standardized sizes makes the kitchen more flexible for menu changes or just for the change over in foods from breakfast to lunch to dinner.

GETTING ORGANIZED

There are lots of innovative storage ideas and hardware to help you organize your kitchen. For the time it will save annually, it is money well spent. On page 89, Sherry once again looked to the restaurant kitchen for inspiration, because even the best restaurant kitchen may not be large or pretty, but it will be well organized.

The ideas learned from a restaurant hold true for home kitchens as well. Having standards helps your kitchen to be flexible. Having the most important items closest at hand will save you time as well by making your kitchen more efficient. You will probably want your favorite frying pan right near the stove. A casserole dish used only for a couple of dishes can be a little farther away, and that fondue pot from the 1970s can be even farther away.

Ease of access can greatly improve the efficiency of a kitchen. Pullout trays, bins, and racks make it much easier to quickly find what you are looking for without pulling everything else out or moving it all around. Divide up drawers to keep the contents separated. Many of these organizational items are available at local home improvement stores and can be installed into pre-existing or new cabinets and drawers.

QUICK TIP

It is a good idea to select your pullouts and divider units before installing the cabinets. It can be easier to install some pullouts and dividers when you can work on all sides of the cabinet. In addition, you might not be able to find a particular unit to fit a particular cabinet, but you might be able to rearrange the size and the configuration of your cabinets to accommodate the unit you want.

PULLOUTS

Pullout storage units can make it much easier to find items stored in a cabinet because when they are pulled out you can examine the entire contents of the cabinet or a portion of the cabinet all at once. Many pullouts will have dividers or sections to help keep everything separated and organized. Pullouts can be vertical and hidden within a cabinet (**Figure 4-16**) or horizontal and hidden within a drawer or cabinet (**Figures 4-17** and **4-18**). They might be attached to the door or drawer front or the cabinet itself.

Some pullouts act as trash bins or large drawers to hold a variety of kitchen supplies and vegetables (**Figures 4-19** to **4-21**). Another kind of pullout is a cutting board that fits just below the countertop but above the top row of drawers (**Figure 4-22**).

Figure 4-16. It is easy to access cooking supplies from both sides of this vertical pullout.

Figure 4-17. This horizontal pullout directly under the cook top is a great spot for utensils, spatulas, spoons, and a favorite frying pan.

Figure 4-18. Opening the cabinet doors under the cook top reveals two pullout drawers that are great for pots, pans, and bowls.

Figure 4-19. This pullout unit provides bins for trash, recycling, or compost.

Figure 4-20. These storage baskets slide out and add an interesting decorative country look to this kitchen.

Figure 4-21. Hidden behind decorative pasta-filled drawer fronts are bins for potatoes and other vegetables.

Figure 4-22. A pullout cutting board just under the countertop adds counter space and provides a convenient spot for slicing bread.

DRAWER DIVIDERS

There are many types of drawer dividers that can be purchased for a variety of uses. The most common type is the old-fashioned silverware holder. These usually slide around because the drawer holding them is never the right size. Many types of dividers are available in a variety of sizes to fit most standard drawers (**Figure 4-23** to **4-26**).

Figure 4-23. This plastic drawer insert for silverware fits the drawer perfectly and will not slide around.

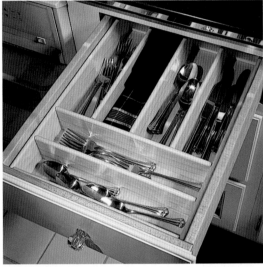

Figure 4-24. Wooden dividers for utensils can be cut to fit any size drawer.

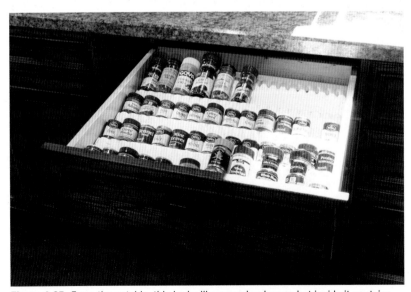

Figure 4-25. From the outside, this looks like a regular drawer, but inside it contains a plastic insert that holds spices conveniently near the cook top unit.

Figure 4-26. A plastic drawer insert for knives not only protects the knives, it prevents injuries by placing the sharp edges down.

DOORS WITH SHELVING

Mount small shelving on the inside of a door (**Figure 4-27**). This is a great space saver in a small kitchen and makes access to small items and spices easy. The shelves in the cabinet may have to be cut back slightly to make room for the shelves in the door. Adding a lot of weight to the door may require installation of reinforced or heavy duty hinges. Utilize the space in front of a sink, as well for sponges and soap, eliminating these messy items from being on the countertop (**Figure 4-28**).

Figure 4-27. Door-mounted shelving is convenient, but you may have to cut back on the shelves in the cabinet to get it to fit.

Figure 4-28. A faux drawer in front of the sink is actually a flip-down holder for sponges and soap.

CHAPTER 5

Tear Out & Construction

Once you have a plan for your new kitchen, work can begin. The first step is probably the messiest—tearing out and disposing of your old cabinets, appliances, and, in some cases, ceiling, and floor. So, spend some time figuring out how you are going to survive without a working kitchen.

The next step is to look at the existing walls and ceilings and see what might need some repair work. This is also a good time to upgrade any plumbing and electrical.

Finally, the work can begin on your new kitchen. On pages 101 to 103, I have included a checklist of the *Order of Work* to give you some guidance about what should come before what to keep a smooth workflow.

HOW TO LIVE IN A CONSTRUCTION ZONE

If you are living in the home at the same time you are remodeling, you may need to keep your kitchen functioning as long as possible. Dining out for every meal quickly gets expensive. We kept our kitchen functional throughout almost the entire remodeling process (**Figure 5-1**). There are a few ways to make this happen:

First, have the old sink, dishwasher, and refrigerator be the last things removed and the new appliances the first things installed. Wash dishes in a nearby sink for the short time the kitchen sink is disconnected.

Second, move appliances when you need to work around them. Cover them with plastic during the workday, and uncover them at night when you need to use them. You will notice in our kitchen-remodeling project that some of the new appliances appear at different times during the process. At the beginning, we put together a list of the appliances we wanted. Then when a particular one went on sale, we bought it. We had all of the appliances before placing the cabinet order to ensure *accurate* measurements.

Third, if you have the flexibility to do the work during the warm part of the year, many meals can be prepared on an outdoor grill. Meals prepared in a microwave oven will also reduce the demand for the kitchen.

Finally, keep it clean. You will need to clean up the construction mess each night in order to use the kitchen. This is a good idea even if you do not plan to use the kitchen. Otherwise, dirt, dust, and debris will get all over the house.

Figure 5-1. Despite torn out cabinets, our kitchen remained functional with the basic appliances: a sink, dishwasher, stove, refrigerator, and microwave.

TEAR OUT

Tearing out the old kitchen is probably the messiest part of the job. The biggest expense here may be for disposal. If you do not have a truck or trailer, the most inexpensive and efficient solution may be to rent a roll-off dumpster. The company will drop off the dumpster and then pick it up when it is full. A ten-cubic-yard dumpster is usually big enough for most remodeling projects. There is often a weekly charge as well so it makes sense to schedule things so the dumpster does not sit in your driveway too long. Any hazardous materials will need to be disposed of properly. Consult your local city or county government offices for a list of disposal rules and sites.

It is often a good idea to leave some things in place when tearing out and cover them up rather than removing them. Some types of linoleum and vinyl flooring are difficult to remove and in older homes, the flooring or the adhesive used to hold it down might contain asbestos. Rather than going through the labor and expense of removing this type of flooring, it is customary to cover it with the new flooring.

Ceilings are another area you might want to cover over rather than remove. There will often be insulation directly above a drywall ceiling that will come down while removing the ceiling. If a soffit has been removed, there may be no drywall on the ceiling behind and above it, so these areas may require patching—a difficult process but simpler than covering the entire ceiling. If you plan to cover the ceiling, cut in any electrical wiring, lighting fixtures, or plumbing as needed so the new work covers it.

Treat walls the same as ceilings. Cut pathways into the drywall for plumbing and wiring to shorten the time it takes to finish the drywall (**Figure 5-2**). Repair walls hidden behind cabinets or appliances later using small patches and one coat of drywall compound (**Figure 5-3**).

It makes sense to complete the majority of the plumbing and wiring right after tear out and before any new cabinets go in. The floor can be completed last to both protect the new flooring material and to save money by not covering the areas that will be covered by the cabinets.

Figure 5-2. Cut narrow pathways through the existing drywall to gain access for new electrical and plumbing lines.

Figure 5-3. Patch small areas of drywall hidden behind cabinets with one coat of drywall compound.

Load-bearing Walls

Before removing any walls, determine if the wall you want to remove is a load-bearing wall. A load-bearing wall is one that holds up the roof or the ceiling and possibly the floor above it. Removing load-bearing walls can bring disastrous consequences. The best way to determine if a wall is load bearing is to get into the attic or the floor above it to see if it is supporting anything. Carefully measure over from the corners of the room below and transfer these measurements upstairs.

If any type of rafter, joist, or support rests over the wall, it is a load-bearing wall. Finally, the ceiling joists or wide boards (usually 2 by 10s or 2 by 12s) that run the length of the ceiling above should run parallel with the wall. If these boards are perpendicular or across the wall, then they are most likely resting on the wall and the wall is load bearing. If there is any doubt about removing a wall, consult an architect or licensed contractor before proceeding. There may be a way to add a beam to replace a load-bearing wall, but again, consult a professional to ensure the beam and whatever is supporting it can carry the weight of whatever is above.

SOFFITS

Traditionally, upper cabinets were 30" (762mm) in height and soffits filled in the space between the top of the cabinet and the ceiling (**Figure 5-4**). Lighting often fits inside the soffits as well. Most upper cabinets are still 30" (762mm) in height, but kitchens have become more open, so the area above the cabinets often is uncovered and crown molding placed around the top of the cabinets (**Figure 5-5**).

For increased storage, many styles of cabinets now are available with a height of 36" or 42" (914mm or 1,067mm), which goes nearly to the ceiling. Add crown molding to hide any gap between the top of the cabinet and the ceiling. Another option is to add a row of small cabinets or shelving above the upper cabinets, but if you do so, they may have to be special ordered. Keeping the existing soffit, or building a new one, are options as well.

Figure 5-4. The soffit fills in the space between the top of the upper cabinet and the ceiling.

Figure 5-5. Removing a soffit and adding crown molding gives a kitchen a more open feel.

Ceilings

In some cases, it may make sense to not tear out the old ceiling, but just cover it with a new layer of drywall or another material. That is what I did in our kitchen. It allows you to add lighting and run needed electrical wiring, plumbing pipes, or ductwork, creating the kitchen's infrastructure, which the new ceiling then covers.

If you removed soffits or walls, cover any voids left behind. Attach furring strips to the ceiling to create a level and flat grid work for hanging the drywall. The strips can run parallel with the ceiling joists or perpendicular (**Figure 5-6**).

Our kitchen was very close to 12' (3,658mm) wide, so I used 12' (3,658mm) long sheets of drywall to eliminate the end joints between the sheets. Anywhere that two sheets of drywall meet there will need to be a tape joint. Without the tape, the joint between the two adjacent sheets would

Figure 5-6. Running furring strips all the way across the ceiling gave me a secure, level surface to anchor the new ceiling.

TIPS FROM THE TRADES

Building Permits

The need to obtain a building permit varies from community to community and you should contact your local city or county government office before doing any work. Generally, a homeowner does not need a contractor, plumber, or electrician's license to work on his or her own home. A homeowner adding new wiring should obtain a permit and have the new work inspected. That rule does not apply to someone adding or changing a few fixtures. The rules for licensing of general contractors, plumbers, and electricians vary from state to state.

If the homeowner is adding on to the home—even if they are doing the work themselves—they will have to get a permit for the whole job and have the work inspected. For major projects, the state or municipality where the home is located could require the homeowner to bring the home into compliance with current building codes.

If a bank is financing the project, it may have strict rules on who can do what to the property.

Doing research in advance is important to avoid facing difficulties or delays later in the project.

Figure 5-7. To keep from having to cover the entire ceiling in both the kitchen and the dining area, I added a step between the two areas.

[SPECIAL TERM]

Tape joint: *A joint between two pieces of drywall that is covered with a strip of paper or fiberglass tape and drywall compound (known as mud).*

TIPS FROM THE TRADES

Drywall Lift

To make quick work of covering a ceiling, you may want to consider renting a drywall lift (**Figure 5-8**). Using a drywall lift instead of raising the drywall by hand and using boards to hold it up can cut the work time in half. It really eliminates the physical work of installing a ceiling even when using 12' (3.7m) long sheets.

Figure 5-8. A rented drywall lift can be a real back and time saver when installing large sheets of drywall.

crack along its length. Each sheet of drywall has a recessed area along its length to create a trough for taping. There is usually no such trough on the ends of drywall sheets. When taping an end joint, feather out the lump along the end of the joint—an onerous but necessary task to be sure. To avoid the problem, keep end joints to a minimum.

For the transition between my kitchen and eat-in dining area, I made a step and covered it with a strip of molding. The step and molding strip prevented me from having to recover the entire ceiling in both rooms. I moved the step out just a bit so it would align with the end of the run of cabinets. This helped create more of a visual transition between the rooms, as well (**Figure 5-7**).

Order of Work

There are a lot of different methods and sequences to go about remodeling an existing kitchen. The following are the steps I usually follow to get the job done.

❑ **1.** Remove all cabinets except the sink cabinet if you plan to continue using the kitchen.

❑ **2.** Remove soffits or walls and rebuild any walls as needed.

❑ **3.** Determine the placement of cabinets on the walls and floor. Use rough measurements made with a level and a measuring tape. Draw in precise level lines when installing the cabinets.

❑ **4.** Stub in all of the electric. *Stubbing* refers to getting all of the wiring from the source to the cans or boxes in the walls and ceilings for planned outlets, switches, and light fixtures. Install any recessed lighting at this time as well.

❑ **5.** Stub in all plumbing.

❑ **6.** Move and/or install all HVAC lines and duct work.

❑ **7.** Install ceiling if needed.

❑ **8.** Patch, repair, and finish all drywall.

❑ **9.** Prepare subfloor if needed. Install final flooring at the end of the project to save money and protect it. (Note: If you are using the same floor, cover it while work is ongoing to protect it.)

❑ **10.** Remove sink cabinet if you have not already.

❑ **11.** Paint the walls. You can paint all of the walls or just exposed areas left following cabinet installation.

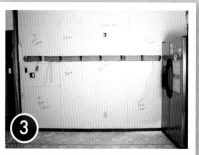

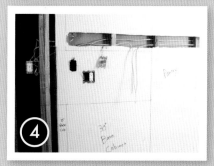

Order of Work (continued)

❑ **12.** Install organizers and sink into cabinets.

❑ **13.** Cut holes in the backs of cabinets for plumbing.

❑ **14.** Shoot a level line around the room.

❑ **15.** Install cabinets.

❑ **16.** Install crown molding.

❑ **17.** Install appliances.

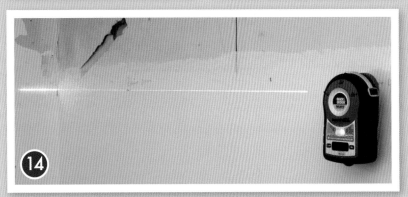

Order of Work *(continued)*

- ❏ **18.** Install counter tops.
- ❏ **19.** Install backsplashes.
- ❏ **20.** Install electrical outlets and fixtures.
- ❏ **21.** Install plumbing and fixtures.
- ❏ **22.** Install flooring.
- ❏ **23.** Install toe kicks.
- ❏ **24.** Install drawer and door pulls.
- ❏ **25.** Touch up paint.

Cabinet Installation

Following delivery of your purchased cabinets, you will be eager to get started. Before doing anything, though, go through and double-check that all of the cabinets you ordered arrived. Use your kitchen layout drawing as a guide.

Assuming the cabinets are *fully assembled* and not *ready to assemble* (RTA), you will need somewhere to store them while you work. Depending on the size and shape of your kitchen, you may just be able to store them on one side of the kitchen and work around them. However, I find it easier to bring them in one or two at a time, install those, and then move on to another set. It is also extremely useful to have a good helper to move the cabinets around and install them. You can do it yourself, but it is not the easiest job. Lower cabinets can be quite heavy.

TOOLS

Next, be sure you have all of the tools needed to do the installation. A tool list usually includes any special tools for your particular cabinets. The list below is a good starting point.

[SPECIAL TERM]

Laser level: *A tool that combines a spirit level and a plumb bob with a laser to shoot a straight beam of light that displays an accurate horizontal or vertical line on the surface. Contractors traditionally use laser levels mounted on a tripod in the center of the room or right to the wall. Today's homeowner models are available for under $40 and are adequate for installing cabinets and countertops. They will even bend around a corner.*

QUICK TIP

If you are installing your cabinets before your flooring, be sure to allow for the thickness of the flooring material you plan to use when determining your top point.

- Safety goggles
- Framing square
- Hammer
- Deadblow or rubber mallet
- Pry bar
- Phillips and flathead screwdrivers
- Level and/or laser level
- Tape measure
- Pencil
- Straight edge
- Electric drill
- Drill bit set
- Countersink bit
- Screwdriver bit
- Extension cord
- Clamps or C-clamps
- Stud finder
- 6' stepladder
- Wood shims
- Scrap lumber (for propping stick or T-brace)
- Circuit tester

FINDING LEVEL

If you are installing cabinets in an older home, chances are the floor and walls have settled somewhat. Even in new homes, the floor may not be exactly level. For cabinets, it is crucial they be level in all directions. Otherwise, the doors may fall open or will not stay open, or the drawers may roll in or out on their own. Countertops also need to be level to prevent objects and liquids from rolling off. The home for our kitchen (shown here) was 40 years old and the kitchen had settled over an inch from one side of the 12'-wide room to the other.

In addition to being level, the counters should all be the same height all the way around the room (unless you are building a kitchen with special needs). In my kitchen, having the counters the same height was particularly important because the end of the peninsula and the nearby counter are so close together. For these reasons, there needs to be a set reference point for everything in the room.

The best place to start is the highest corner. Then use shims to raise cabinets installed away from the highest corner to keep them all at the same height. It would be very difficult to start at the lowest point and then cut the cabinets down as the floor rises up.

To determine the highest corner, start by laying out an initial line on the wall around the room. One way to do this is to use a laser level (**Figure 6-1**). Measure down to find the smallest dimension between this line and the floor. This indicates the highest point of the floor—your starting point.

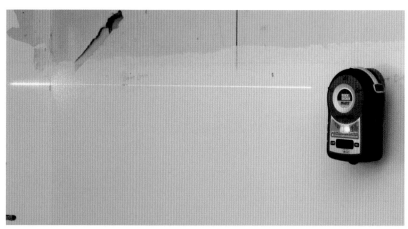

Figure 6-1. A laser level shoots out a beam of light that bends around a corner.

Figure 6-2. The laser level has a mounting bracket with a nail that goes into the drywall right on the reference marks.

Starting at the highest corner, use the laser line, a pencil, and a straightedge to mark a reference line around the room at a convenient height. Reference all other measurements from this line.

Next, refer to your design layout to determine the top point of your upper cabinets. Then, still working at the highest corner, measure up from the floor to this top point and make a mark on the wall.

Measure down and mark the bottom of the upper cabinets and the top of the lower cabinets, and locate the laser level on these marks (**Figure 6-2**). Use a pencil and a straightedge to extend the lines around to the wall surfaces where the cabinets will be located (**Figure 6-3**).

While marking the horizontal reference lines on the wall, it is a good time to locate wall studs that will be used to hang and secure the cabinets. You can do this with a stud finder, looking for electrical outlets or nail locations, and remembering that studs are usually located 16" (406mm) on center (**Figure 6-4**).

Figure 6-3. Use a pencil to extend the lines around the room and label all of your lines (i.e. *Bottom of Upper Cabinet*) with a pencil or masking tape label to keep everything straight.

[SPECIAL TERM]

Stud finder: *A handheld device with a small radar system used to determine the location of the edges of wood and metal framing studs hidden behind the drywall.*

Figure 6-4. Here I am locating wall studs to hang the cabinets. Note how I have also labeled the location and size of each cabinet.

THE FIRST CABINET

After unboxing and unwrapping the first cabinet, check it closely for any damages. Remove any loose shelves and drawers to lighten the load. Be sure to put any loose hardware in a container so it will not get lost.

Okay, which comes first? Hanging the upper cabinets or installing the lower cabinets? I usually hang the upper cabinets first; otherwise, the deeper lower cabinets get in the way. However, the cabinets are heavy so this method usually will require a helper to get them up and secured to the wall. If you don't have a helper, you can install the lower cabinets first then make a small framework or box that sits on top of the lower cabinets for the upper cabinets to rest on while they are being fastened to the wall.

I started hanging the cabinets in my original reference corner. With reference lines drawn around the kitchen, though, you can start from another fixed point, such as the stove or another fixed appliance, near a door or window, or over the sink. Leave any areas where there will be gaps between cabinets or against the wall until last because those dimensions can vary. Fill gaps and spaces later (see the description for scribing on page 113.)

Using the stud locations determined earlier, transfer the measurements to the top and back of the cabinet (**Figure 6-5**). Then drill holes for #10 x 2½" (64mm) panhead hanging screws (or the screws specified for your cabinets) through the hanging rails. Depending upon the type of hanging rail your cabinets have, the holes might be located inside or above the cabinet. For cabinets with a thicker back, the screws can go anywhere through the back.

Figure 6-5. Using the inside measurements of a framing square, transfer the locations of the wall studs to the cabinet. If possible, try to attach the cabinet to at least two studs.

Figure 6-6. Using the pre-marked lines as reference, Kevan and I placed the first upper-corner cabinet.

Unless you use a *French Cleat* system (see *Tips from the Trades* on page 110), you will most likely need an assistant to help hang the upper cabinets. My friend Kevan Stratton was good enough to help me out with this project (**Figure 6-6**).

Once in position, drive a panhead screw through the hanging rail (or cabinet back) and into the stud in the wall. (Note: The screw should be long enough to go through the back of the cabinet and the wallboard then penetrate the stud by at least 1½" [38mm]). The panhead acts as a washer to prevent the screw head from going right through the back of the cabinet.

QUICK TIP

Before hanging the cabinets, be certain any wiring for undercabinet lighting is free and clear of the back of the cabinet. You can either drill a hole in the back of the cabinet for the wires or just bring them in under the bottom edge of the cabinet.

QUICK TIP

Even with an assistant, sometimes it is easiest to temporarily screw a piece of straight scrap to the wall as a rest right at the bottom of the cabinet. This helps keep everything level and in position while the screws are being driven into the studs.

LEVELING THE FIRST CABINET

It is crucial that the cabinets are all level and plumb because you want to work with gravity rather than against it to make sure the cabinet doors do not fall open or swing closed unintentionally. A simple measurement up from the floor, down from the ceiling, or out from a wall will not work because the floors, ceilings, and walls are most likely not level or plumb to begin with.

With the first screw in place, use a bubble level to check across the top of the cabinet. Once the cabinet is level, drive a second or third screw along the top and bottom borders anywhere that you can hit a stud (**Figure 6-7**).

Next, check if the cabinet is plumb (**Figure 6-8**). If the cabinet is not plumb vertically, you will have to shim it. Most lumberyards and home improvement stores carry wooden shims or you can use cedar roof shingles. If the top needs to come out to make the cabinet plumb, you will have to loosen the screws slightly along the top and place shims near the screws to bring the top out from the wall. If the bottom needs to come out, place your shims near the bottom (**Figures 6-9** and **6-10**). It is crucial to get the first cabinet plumb and level because the remaining cabinets attach to it. Try opening the door to make sure it does not swing closed. Then close it to make sure it does not fall open.

Once the cabinet is level and plum, tighten up the screws snug (do not over-tighten), and check it one more time. Then cut off the shims even with the cabinet by scoring them with a knife or saw and breaking them off cleanly.

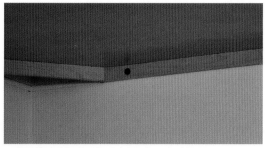

Figure 6-7. Here a screw is added along the bottom rail of the cabinet and into a wall stud.

Figure 6-8. I am using a bubble level to check for plumb. The level indicates the cabinet needs to come out a little bit at the bottom.

Figure 6-9. Driving a wooden shim between the cabinet and the wall near the bottom of the cabinet seems to solve the problem.

Figure 6-10. Driving shims up from the bottom of the cabinet also is an option.

[SPECIAL TERM]

Plumb: *A vertical line or plane that can be determined by a reading from a bubble level, a laser level, or a plumb bob.*

QUICK TIP

To determine if a hung cabinet is level and plumb, place a marble or round pencil inside the cabinet to see if it rolls in one direction.

ADDING CABINETS

With the first upper cabinet securely in place, it is a matter of adding the remaining upper cabinets one at a time. As on the first cabinet, pre-drill screw holes for hanging that will align with the wall studs. Then lift the cabinet into position and clamp the face frames of the two cabinets together (**Figure 6-13**). Next, check that the cabinet is level and plumb just as you did on the first cabinet (**Figure 6-14**).

Once the cabinet is in position, drill two ³⁄₃₂" (2.5mm) pilot holes through the face frames—one near the top and one near the bottom. The holes should be deep enough to go through the

Figure 6-13. Securely clamp the two cabinets together with a couple of clamps, checking that the face frames join at the front without any gap.

TIPS FROM THE TRADES

A French Cleat System

One method to securely and simply fasten an upper cabinet to the wall is to use a *French Cleat* system. This involves screwing a hanging cleat to the wall with a 45° angle cut along its top and a mating cleat fastened to the back of the cabinet (**Figure 6-11**). Then, add a shim to the wall near the bottom of the cabinet and a filler strip at the bottom of the cabinet. Now it is simple to just set the cabinet over the angled cleat (**Figure 6-12**). The cleat will easily support the weight of the cabinet and is a great system to use if you are trying to hang an upper cabinet by yourself. The only downside is there will be a gap on the side of the cabinet at the back. The gap is hidden if the cabinet abuts another cabinet or appliance. If it is on an open end, a vertical strip of molding or an end cap easily covers the gap.

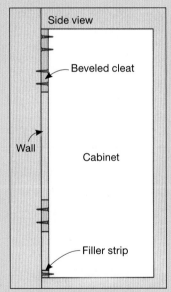

Figure 6-11. A French cleat system uses a pair of beveled cleats that mate. One attaches to the wall and one attaches to the back of the cabinet. Add a filler strip near the bottom.

Figure 6-12. With the beveled cleats in place, it is easy for one person to lift the cabinet up and rest it down on the cleat attached to the wall. Use a shim attached to the wall for additional support for the cabinet back.

first frame and slightly into the second frame. I like to use a piece of tape on the drill bit to gauge the depth of each hole (**Figure 6-15**). Then, use a countersink bit so the screw will be flush or slightly below the surface.

With the holes drilled, I drove special frame attachment screws to securely hold the cabinets together (**Figure 6-16**). These screws have smaller *trim heads* that are cleaner in appearance. After securely screwing the cabinets together, drive screws through the hanging rails or the cabinet back and into the wall studs. And, of course, continue to check for plumb and level and shim where necessary.

Figure 6-14. As you add cabinets, always check that they are level and plumb. If they are not, add shims.

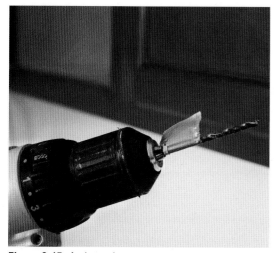

Figure 6-15. A piece of tape serves as a depth gauge when drilling the pilot hole.

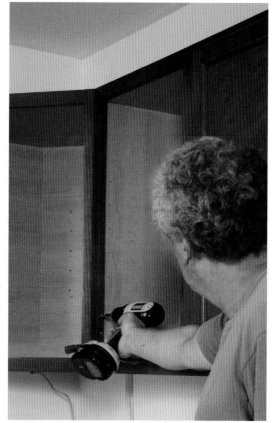

Figure 6-16. I use an electric drill with a square driver bit to drive trim head screws that will hold the cabinets together.

[SPECIAL TERM]

Square driver bit:
Sometimes called a Robertson bit, many trim head screws have a square drive, which allows them to be driven with more power than a conventional Phillips bit. In addition, square drive screws are not as likely to slip or cam out while being driven.

Figure 6-17. Once the pantry cabinet was in place, Kevan used the bubble level to check for plumb.

Figure 6-18. The pantry cabinet was leaning a little forward so I shimmed under the front edge.

Figure 6-19. Simply slide the shim between the cabinet and the floor. Trim the shim later after all of the screws are in place.

Now continue with this process, working your way around the room mounting all of the upper cabinets. If you have any pantry cabinets or other cabinets that run the full height of the upper and lower cabinets, install them now (**Figures 6-17, 6-18** and **6-19**). Fasten any additional cabinets to adjacent fixtures and to the wall using screws at various points to help carry the extra load.

Install wall-mounted appliances at the same time as the wall cabinets. Attach a microwave oven, for example, to the wall and the cabinet above it (**Figure 6-20**). You may also need to cut an opening through the upper cabinet above an oven for venting if the fan is to vent through the roof.

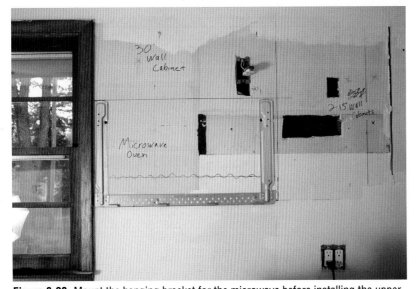

Figure 6-20. Mount the hanging bracket for the microwave before installing the upper cabinets around it. Be certain an electrical plug is in the wall and there is a hole in the cabinet above or beside the microwave for its power cord.

FILLING VOIDS

Unless your cabinets are custom made, there will most likely be a gap or difference in the distance between the combined length of the cabinets and the distance between the walls. Fill the gap using one of the following four methods:

1. One common method for getting a nice tight fit is to use a filler board. The only problem, once again, is that the walls of your house may not be perfectly plumb. For example, there may be a 2" gap between the cabinet and the wall at the bottom and a 2¼" gap at the top. Therefore, you need a tapered filler board that is wider at the top than the bottom. This taper can be cut with a hand plane, handsaw, jig saw, or tapering jig on the table saw.

2. If the run of your cabinets is slightly longer than the distance between the walls, then cut a shape into the face frame of the cabinet. That is one of the reasons why the face frames of your cabinets overlap the sides of the cabinet by at least ¼" (6mm). To get a perfect fit, I like to *scribe* the contour of the wall onto this overhanging face frame. To scribe the wall's contour, position the cabinet slightly away from the adjoining wall. Then use a compass with a pencil (or a divider) to transfer the shape of the wall onto the wood by running one of the compass points along the wall and the pencil on the face frame (**Figure 6-21**). Next, cut the shape made by the pencil with a jig saw or hand plane. Then, sand or file the edge to make a tight gap-free joint between the wall and the face frame. Fill any small gaps with caulk or wood filler.

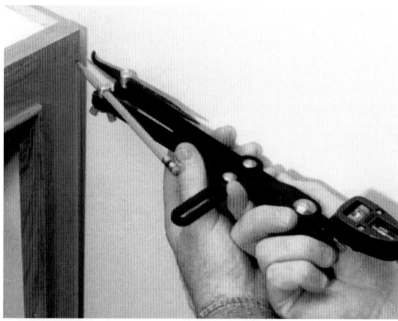

Figure 6-21. Scribe a line that will follow the contour of the mating wall on the face frame of the cabinet using a compass or divider. Then, cut or plane to the line for a tight fit.

QUICK TIP

To fill many types of gaps, open spaces, or toe kicks, most retailers will sell pre-finished wood to match their cabinets.

[SPECIAL TERM]

Scribe: *Marking a cabinet or filler strip using a compass or divider with a line that runs parallel to a mating wall. Cutting to the line will allow a cabinet or filler strip to fit tight against the wall.*

3. If you are using corner cabinets or cabinets that wrap around a corner, you will not be able to scribe the face frame into the sidewall. In that case, you will need to fill a gap between two cabinets somewhere in the center of the run. In our kitchen, I wanted to center the upper cabinets on the window, so I measured out from there. I then made a gap between two cabinets that were off to one side and added a filler there from a backer strip and a thinner facing piece (**Figures 6-22** to **6-25**).

4. The final method for closing a gap is to lap a strip of finished wood over the face frame. If the run of cabinets ends near the adjacent wall, shape the strip to the form of the wall. If the gap is in the middle of the run of cabinets, the strip could also overlap the edge of two cabinets. (Note: If you are planning to run crown molding over the face frame of the cabinets, there is one problem using this method. The solution is to run the crown molding *before* attaching the strips. The strips can then butt up against the bottom of the crown molding.)

Figure 6-22. To fill the gap between cabinets, I started by adding a ¾" (19mm)-thick backing strip. Screw the strip in place from inside the cabinet.

Figure 6-23. Next, I cut a second strip to fit between the cabinets. It was cut to thickness to leave a ¼" (6mm) set back.

Figure 6-24. Then some extra ¼" (6mm)-thick toe kick material was cut to fit between the cabinets and flush with the front of the frame.

Figure 6-25. With the doors in place, the filled gap seems to be a natural part of the cabinet run.

BASE CABINETS

After installing all of the upper cabinets (**Figure 6-26**), it is time to start laying out the base cabinet locations. Install the base cabinets in much the same way as the wall cabinets. Level the base cabinets where necessary with shims and firmly secure them to the wall and floor.

Consider two things in working with the base cabinets: the weight and thickness of the countertop and the thickness of the flooring material. Some countertop materials, such as thick granite or concrete, may require some additional reinforcement to support the additional weight. If it's needed, gain extra support by attaching an additional strip of wood to the wall along the back of the cabinets or adding an additional layer of plywood between or inside the cabinets. In most cases, however, the cabinets themselves should provide enough support for the countertops.

The main thing to remember in installing the base cabinets is you are usually trying to arrive at a standard 36" (914mm) height from the top of the floor to the top of the countertop. I find it easiest to install the base cabinets *before* the floor. For example, if I knew I was going to have a ¾" (19mm)-thick floor, and a 1½" (38mm) thick countertop, the ideal height of my cabinets would be 33¾" (857mm) high (36" minus ¾", minus 1½"= 33¾"). (Note: Don't worry if you are quarter-inch or so too high or low.)

Because I knew which was the highest corner in the kitchen, I decided to begin installing the base cabinets in the same corner as the upper cabinets. Check this corner to see how level the cabinet will be when it is in place. If the floor is extremely unlevel, you may be able to cut a little material away from the bottom of the first cabinet. However, for the most part, it is best to start by

Figure 6-26. With all of the upper cabinets in place, mark the locations of the base cabinets.

Figure 6-27. It is common to have a toe kick area cut out of the sides of a base cabinet.

leveling the first cabinet and raising the rest as necessary using shims.

There are two kinds of cabinets commercially available. Most have a toe kick base already attached or a toe kick area cut out of the sides of the cabinets (**Figure 6-27**). Some cabinets require a separate base or have adjustable metal or plastic legs, see sidebar on page 118. One advantage of a

QUICK TIP

Installing the base cabinets before installing the flooring saves money on flooring.

Figure 6-28. Some cabinets, such as this long run, require a separate base secured to both the floor and the cabinets.

Figure 6-29. I shimmed the lazy Susan corner units to the same height as the other base cabinets.

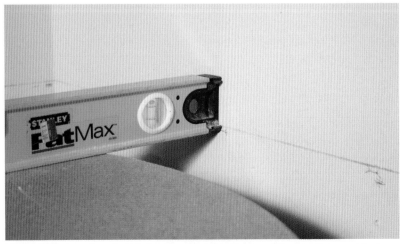

Figure 6-30. I used my bubble level to make sure the top of the lazy Susan cabinet would be the correct height in relation to my layout line on the wall.

separate base is you can usually make it yourself. Changing the height of the base allows for more variance in the height of the countertops and more leeway for an uneven floor. Level the bases, though, and secure them to the floor before installing the cabinets (**Figure 6-28**).

The cabinets I chose for this kitchen had the bases already attached so a separate base was not required. One example is the corner lazy Susan cabinets I used to fit in the corners of my kitchen. Some lazy Susan cabinets have sides, but this particular type did not. The cabinets themselves are circular with a pie-shaped piece cut out of the front corner (**Figure 6-29**). I purchased cabinets with a base, which required leveling and trimming to the correct height (**Figure 6-30**).

The lazy Susan units also took a bit of measuring to get them positioned correctly (**Figure 6-31**). Then once again I checked the cabinet for plumb (**Figure 6-32**) and level shimming when necessary.

Now that the corner unit is in place, you can continue by attaching the adjacent cabinets always checking for plumb (**Figure 6-33**) and level (**Figure 6-34**). After each cabinet is plumbed and leveled with shims, screw it tightly to the wall, trying to catch at least two studs per cabinet (**Figure 6-35**). Then clamp each adjacent cabinet to the previous one across the face frames, and drill and screw them together with trim head screws (**Figure 6-36**).

If you are installing base cabinets with a toe kick base as part of the cabinet and there is a bottom in the cabinet, you may not be able to attach the cabinet to the floor. Securing the cabinets to the wall and fastening them together will offer enough support in most cases. Some base cabinets have a hanging strip for the screws to secure the cabinet to the wall. Other base

Figure 6-31. I used a tape measure to be certain the lazy Susan unit was the correct distance from the wall and aligned with the other base cabinets. Notice the shims under the front edges to level the unit.

Figure 6-32. Before I tightened all of the screws, I checked the cabinet for plumb and shimmed where needed.

Figure 6-33. After positioning the adjacent cabinet, I checked it for plumb.

Figure 6-34. Then I checked the cabinet for level and tapped in shims under the front edge where necessary.

Figure 6-35. After adding each cabinet, I clamped the face frames together and attached the cabinet to the wall.

Figure 6-36. To hold the cabinets together tightly, clamp the face frames so they are perfectly flush across their faces. Then drill and screw them together with three screws.

Adjustable Legs

A different technique for building a base under a cabinet has become popular recently because it is easy to level and allows access under cabinets. It involves four little plastic adjustable legs that give you a range from 3¹¹⁄₁₆" (78mm) to 5⅞" (149mm) high (**Figure 6-39**). The toe kick face has clips attached to the back that snap onto the legs (**Figure 6-40**). This makes the toe kick removable for easy access to plumbing and electrical lines. These adjustable leg levelers are load rated at 400 pounds per foot and available from *www.Rockler.com* .

cabinets have a thick enough back that they can be secured to the wall anywhere in the back. That was the case in the new cabinets in our kitchen (**Figure 6-37**).

Add filler boards between base cabinets where necessary just like on the upper cabinets. Be certain there is room for all of the appliances (**Figure 6-38**). Add the toe kick facing after installing the floor.

> **QUICK TIP**
> When inserting shims in the back of the cabinet, make sure they are near the screws to prevent the back from bending.

Figure 6-37. When a cabinet has a thick back and no hanging rail such as the new ones in our kitchen, place the screws anywhere you can easily find wall studs.

Figure 6-39. Use adjustable leveler legs to replace traditional toe kick bases.

Mounting screw

Cap

Toe kick clip

Adjustable stem

Foot pad

Mounting plate

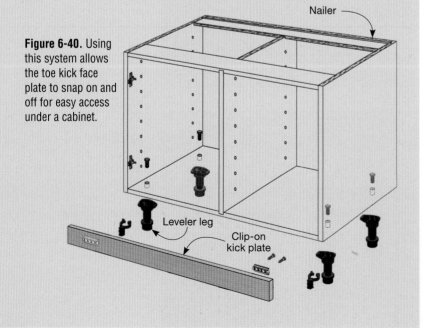

Figure 6-40. Using this system allows the toe kick face plate to snap on and off for easy access under a cabinet.

Nailer

Leveler leg

Clip-on kick plate

Figure 6-38. All of the base cabinets and appliances (refrigerator, dishwasher, and stove) fit perfectly.

ALTERING BASE CABINETS

You may find the particular type or style of cabinet you need is not available in the style or color that you want. In our kitchen, I needed a sink cabinet narrower than the typical sink cabinet so the dishwasher would fit where I wanted it. There are three possible solutions to the problem. First, you can build a cabinet from scratch (That can be time consuming and getting a perfect color match can be difficult). Second, you can order a custom-sized cabinet from the manufacturer (That is expensive). Therefore, my choice is usually to buy an existing cabinet and alter it.

Sink cabinets are usually available in a limited range of sizes. Base cabinets, however, are available in many more sizes so I ordered a base cabinet that would fit the space. The only problem is base cabinets do not have an opening in the back that allows for the installation of plumbing and they usually have drawers near the top that would interfere with a sink. The simple solution here was to cut out an opening in the back of the base cabinet I ordered and remove the drawer fronts from the drawers. Then later I reattached the fronts to the face of the cabinet.

I started by removing the drawers and drawer hardware (**Figure 6-41**). I also had to cut out a shelf with a jigsaw (Note: Watch out for screws, nails, and staples). At this point, I discovered the sink I wanted to install was just a little too big to fit into the opening (**Figure 6-42**). All I had to do to get it to fit was trim a little out of the corner gussets (**Figure 6-43**). Then the sink fit perfectly (**Figure 6-44**).

[SPECIAL TERM]

Gusset: *A triangular-shaped piece of wood usually attached in a corner of the cabinet to add strength and rigidity.*

Figure 6-41. First, remove the drawers, hardware, and any shelves. (Note the plumbing and electrical outlet on the wall behind the cabinet.)

Figure 6-42. I marked the area for removal from each corner gusset so the sink would fit.

Figure 6-43. I cut out the marked area of each gusset with a jigsaw.

Figure 6-44. Here the sink is just about to fit into the opening. After cutting out a little more, it set down tight against the top of the cabinet (and later, the countertop).

[SPECIAL TERM]

Forstner bit: *A drill bit with a sharp rim that cuts a clean (usually large) hole.*

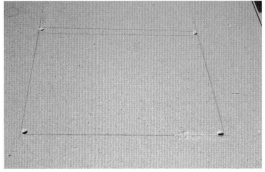

Figure 6-45. I carefully laid the cabinet down on its front and marked an opening in the back that will accept the pipes and the electrical outlet. Then I drilled holes at each corner of the opening.

The next steps were to cut out the back of the cabinet to accommodate the plumbing and an electrical outlet (**Figures 6-45** to **6-49**). This involved marking and cutting the opening, drilling out a hole for a large pipe, and cutting some notches for smaller pipes.

To maintain the design of the cabinets, you should reattach the drawer fronts to the front of the sink cabinet. It will still look like there are drawers, but there are not any (because of the sink). To do this, I added a support board behind the face frame (**Figures 6-50** to **6-53**).

Figure 6-46. Next, I cut out the opening with my jigsaw.

Figure 6-47. A larger pipe needed to come through the back at a distance from the main opening, so I drilled out another hole with a large Forstner bit.

Figure 6-48. The hot and cold water pipes came up through the floor. I laid out notches and then cut them out with my jigsaw.

Figure 6-49. With the large opening, notches, and hole complete, I pushed the cabinet back in place over the plumbing and attached it to the wall.

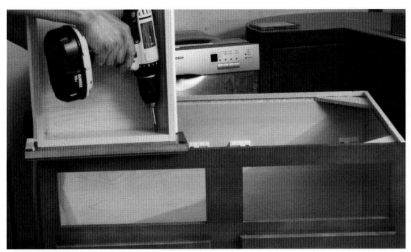

Figure 6-50. The first step is to remove the drawer fronts from the drawer boxes. I used a drill with a driver bit and ran it in reverse.

Figure 6-51. Next, I cut a support board to fit behind the drawer openings and clamped it to the face frame.

Figure 6-52. Next, I drilled and screwed the support board to the face frame from the back. Finally, I screwed the drawer fronts to the support board from the back with the original screws that held the fronts to the drawer boxes.

Figure 6-53. The altered cabinet fits in place perfectly and follows the design of the rest of the kitchen. Pulls could be added to the fronts of the faux drawers, but then users could not stand up tight against the cabinet while working at the sink.

The other cabinet I needed to alter was for the peninsula bar that divides the kitchen from the dining room. I wanted to be able to reduce its depth so that I could fit a couple of stools under the bar. This was a little more work but anyone with some basic woodworking experience could do this as well. I started by cutting through the cabinet side and bottom with my portable circular saw and a fence (**Figures 6-54** to **6-57**). Make sure there are no nails, staples, or screws in the path of the blade.

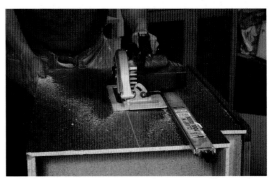

Figure 6-54. To position the fence for cutting the peninsula bar cabinet narrower, measure the distance from the edge of the saw base to the inside of the blade.

TIPS FROM THE TRADES

Shelf Pin Drilling Bit

Shelf pins support the shelves in most kitchen cabinets. The pins fit into holes drilled into the inside of the cabinet. If you alter a cabinet (as I did to make the peninsula bar), you will probably have to drill new shelf pin holes and cut the shelves narrower. One way to get the holes accurately aligned is to use a shelf pin drilling jig (**Figure 6-63**). Lay the jig down on the side of the cabinet with the holes lined up over the existing holes to check the orientation of the holes and the jig. Then move the jig over to the opposite position in the cabinet and drill the shelf pin holes. If you do not have a jig, you can accurately measure and mark the location of the holes and then use a bit the same size as your shelf pins.

Figure 6-55. Secure the fence the same dimension from the cut line and saw through the side of the cabinet. You may also use a straight board and a couple of clamps as a fence.

Figure 6-56. By making the cut deep, it also starts the cut for the bottom of the cabinet.

Figure 6-63. A shelf pin drilling jig with a special drill bit helps align and drill holes for shelf pins accurately in relation to each other.

Figure 6-57. To cut the bottom of the cabinet, I screwed a board to the bottom panel as a guide. Finish the cut with a hand saw if necessary.

After cutting the sides and the bottom to their final width, I nailed the back in place through the sides (**Figure 6-58**) and the back (**Figure 6-59**). Then I shortened up the drawers and reattached the backs. Finally, new shorter slides finished the drawers (**Figure 6-60**), I attached cherry plywood to the backs of the cabinets (**Figure 6-61** and **6-62**).

Figure 6-58. I used my air nailer to reattach the back of the cabinet to the sides. You could pre-drill small holes and drive finishing nails with a hammer and nail set. Afterward, I covered the holes with corner molding.

Figure 6-59. I also nailed through the back of the cabinet and into the bottom.

Figure 6-60. With the drawers cut short and new sides added—this photograph shows the finished peninsula from the kitchen side.

Figure 6-61. I cut and nailed cherry plywood to the back of the peninsula bar cabinet and the lazy Susan cabinet in the corner. Later, I added some trim corner molding around each outside corner.

Figure 6-62. Here you can see the completed peninsula bar from the dining room side. Two stools fit neatly under the counter.

CROWN MOLDING

In addition to providing an attractive finish detail to a kitchen, sometimes a piece of crown molding can hide a gap where a tall cabinet reaches the ceiling or soffit. That was not the case in our kitchen. All of the cabinets are set down from the ceiling, so I used crown molding just as decoration **(Figure 6-64).**

There are a few things you need to know about crown molding. First, end-to-end joints are hard to conceal so it often is available in 12-foot lengths. Next, you can make it yourself if you have a shaper or router table, but it may be easier to just buy it, and there are a variety of designs available (**Figure 6-65**).

Some stock cabinets have matching crown molding available for them. Alternatively, you may be able to find crown molding in pine or poplar and then stain or paint it to match your cabinets. It is also available in solid plastic or foam covered with veneer or plastic.

The decorative part of the crown molding always faces out (the front) with a flat surface and two narrow 45° bevels (called *flats*) along the back face (**Figure 6-66**).

QUICK TIP

Always apply crown molding with the cove detail or dentil (small evenly spaced blocks of wood) facing down.

Figure 6-64. Crown molding adds a decorative touch to the top of all of the upper cabinets.

Figure 6-65. Crown moldings are available in a variety of sizes and shapes.

Figure 6-66. Though the front face of different crown moldings may vary, the back face (here facing down) has a flat surface and two 45° bevels (flats).

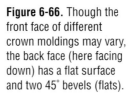

Cutting Crown Molding

Use a power miter saw to cut crown molding to length on the job site. When cutting outside corners, the ends where the two pieces of molding meet are cut with the molding tilted at the same angle in relation to the blade as it will be in relation to the face of the cabinet— with one important difference. The molding should sit on top of the saw upside down (**Figure 6-67**). I like to draw pencil marks on the base of the miter saw to keep the angle of the crown molding to the proper angle to the wall. You will need to make two marks on the part of the saw table that rotates (**Figure 6-68**). Be sure that when you make the marks, both faces of the 45° bevels are resting flat on the saw table and the fence. To check the accuracy of the set-up, cut two scraps of molding, a left hand and right hand side, then hold or tape them together and lay them down on your bench top or on the front of a cabinet to make sure that the corner is 90° and the up and down angle looks correct. If it looks off, change your pencil lines.

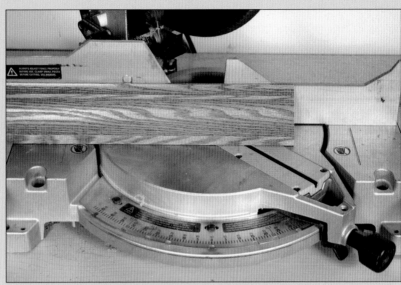

Figure 6-67. When cutting miters on crown molding, tilt the molding against the saw's table and fence to match the way it will fit in relation to the cabinet–but upside down.

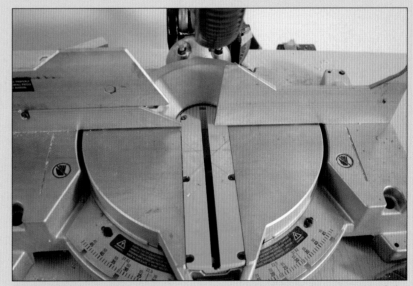

Figure 6-68. With pencil marks going both directions, the saw is set up to cut angled to the right or left.

QUICK TIP

When nailing molding in place, using an air nailer (brad or pin) makes the job go quicker and prevents the molding from splitting. If you do not have access to an air nailer, you may want to pre-drill holes before driving and set the nails with a nail set to prevent splitting. Use one-inch nails so they do not come out through the back of the frame into the cabinet.

Figure 6-69. To prevent a gap from appearing when adding crown molding, I nailed on a piece of pre-finished material that came with my cabinets. The crown molding hides the nails.

To cut and attach the crown molding to the cabinets in our kitchen I started from the left end and worked my way around the room clockwise. However, I had an immediate problem. The face frame of the first cabinet extended slightly out from the side of the cabinet and it would leave a gap. To solve the problem, I nailed on a thin strip of wood that was the same thickness (⅜" [10mm] in my case) as the face frame extension (**Figure 6-69**).

To fit the first piece of crown molding into the wall, hold the molding at the proper angle and transfer the shape or angle of the wall to the molding (**Figure 6-70**).

Next, mark the underside of the crown molding right where the corners of the cabinet meet and cut the first miter. This is where you will use the reference lines on the saw. (Remember to cut the piece in the upside down position!) After cutting the first piece, nail it in place (**Figure 6-71**).

To cut the miter for the second piece of molding, rotate the saw to the opposing 45° setting and cut a miter to meet the first piece of molding.

Figure 6-70. Because most walls are not flat or vertical, scribe the end of the molding and cut it to the pencil line with the molding laying flat on the miter saw.

Figure 6-71. To maintain proper orientation to the cabinet, use a level when nailing the molding in place.

Then measure its length (short point-to-short point) by holding the molding in position on the cabinet and marking where the bottom of the crown molding meets the cabinet. Once again, rotate the saw, and cut the second piece to length.

Now, to help keep the joint together, apply some glue to the ends of both pieces and nail the first and second pieces together (**Figure 6-72**).

Follow the same process for all of the outside corner joints. The best appearance for an *inside* corner joint is to use a technique known as *coping* (instead of just cutting two 45˚ miters). A coped corner always seems to look more natural even though it takes a little more time and effort.

To begin a coped inside corner, install the end of one of the pieces with the end cut straight. (That is, cut it at 90˚, not 45˚.) (**Figure 6-73**). Next, to determine the length of the other piece, measure out from the bottom edge of the first piece, not the original corner. This is where the second piece actually starts.

Coping Inside Corner

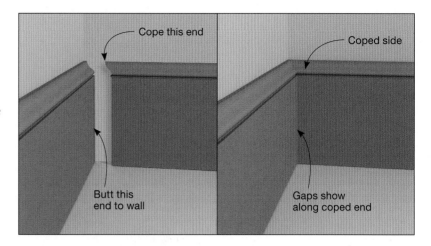

Cope this end
Butt this end to wall
Coped side
Gaps show along coped end

Before coping the end of the piece, it is a good idea to map out the profile of the crown molding to use as a guide. To do this, cut a *backward* miter on the miter saw by setting the saw to 45˚, placing the workpiece with the good face *out* on the saw, and making a cut (**Figure 6-74**). This fresh edge provides a visual reference when coping.

Now it is time to do the actual coping. Tilt the coping saw slightly inward to undercut the molding. Then, follow the contour of the profile

[SPECIAL TERM]

Coping: *Shaping the end of a piece of molding by cutting it with a coping saw or scroll saw so it will fit tight against another piece of molding at an inside corner.*

Figure 6-73. The first piece of molding on an inside corner is cut at 90˚ and nailed in position.

Figure 6-72. To secure the joints, apply glue to the ends of both pieces, and then nail them together.

Figure 6-74. Cut a backward miter on the miter saw to provide a visual map for coping.

QUICK TIP

Cut the backward miter on an extra-long piece of molding in case you make a mistake when coping. Then, there is extra material to miter and try again.

as closely as possible. The undercut will help to ensure a tight gap-free joint between the two pieces (**Figure 6-75**).

Continue cutting along the line made by the miter saw as far as you can without twisting the blade too much. If necessary, start cutting in from

Figure 6-75. Use the profile from the miter cut as a guide when coping with a coping saw.

the other side of the molding in order to reach all of the details. Because it can be difficult to get an exact cut with the coping saw, use files, rasps, and sandpaper to refine the shape of the end. You will probably need to put the two pieces together a few times and test them to make sure the fit is tight (**Figure 6-76**).

Once it fits without gaps (**Figure 6-77**), glue and nail the second piece of molding in place (**Figure 6-78**).

Note: For the corner cabinets, the inside joints look fine if they are mitered and not coped. That is because the angle is 45˚, not 90˚ (**Figure 6-79**).

Figure 6-76. As you work, test fit the cut frequently to the mating profile to obtain a tight fit.

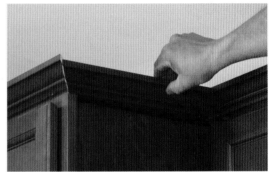

Figure 6-77. The coped piece should fit tight into the inside corner joint without any gaps.

Figure 6-78. Apply some glue on the end of the coped molding and then nail it into place.

Figure 6-79. On the corner cabinets, the angle is 45˚ so you can simply cut a miter and save a lot of coping.

HANDLES AND PULLS

Finishing touches such as door handles and drawer pulls can really help to complement the design of your kitchen. There is a range of styles, colors, and sizes from which to choose. Cheap inexpensive handles and pulls can bring down the quality of good cabinets, but good quality handles can add to the quality of inexpensive cabinets. Do not cut corners on handles. Avoid making them look like an afterthought by spending some time choosing them at the same time you are picking the cabinets. This will help to create a more unified design (**Figure 6-80**).

Handles and pulls, commonly made of metal, wood, or ceramic material, come in an almost unlimited variety of styles, shapes, and sizes.

When you select the size and style for your kitchen, consider how they will complement the look of the rest of the kitchen. Make sure, for example, that the style matches the hinges. Also, consider how easy they will be to grab and open the doors and drawers, and to keep clean. Ornate handles and pulls may look nice but they tend to catch dirt and the clothing of people leaning against or walking by the cabinet. Wooden handles can be difficult to clean unless they have a durable finish on them.

There are a few standard dimensions in the manufacturing of handles and pulls that make them easier to mount and replace if you would like a different style. First, most have either one or two

Figure 6-80. Choosing quality door handles and drawer pulls will add to the overall appearance of your kitchen.

Building an Alignment Jig

To lay out and drill consistently spaced holes for door handles, I like to build a little jig out of scrap wood. It consists of a base piece and two small fences that hook over the corner of the door (**Figure 6-82**). The jig has two pre-drilled holes that correspond to the distance between the screw holes in the door pull. To use the jig, clamp it securely to the door and drill through the pre-drilled holes and through the door (**Figure 6-83**). The position of the holes in the door should perfectly match the screw holes in the handle (**Figure 6-84**). (Note: To accommodate a set of doors, you will need to build both a right and a left hand jig.) It takes a little time to make and carefully lay out the jig, but accuracy makes it well worth the effort. Use the same jig to drill handle holes in doors already mounted on the cabinet (**Figure 6-85**).

Figure 6-82. A shop-built hardware-locating jig fits over the corner of the door.

Figure 6-83. When clamping the jig in place be sure the fences are tight against the door. Then drill through both holes in the jig and through the door. To prevent the wood from splitting outward on the back of the door, hold or clamp a scrap piece of wood under the door.

Figure 6-84. The jig guarantees perfect hole locations for attaching the handle.

Figure 6-85. The same jig can be used to drill holes in a door that is already mounted on the cabinet.

machine screws to attach the handle or pull to the door or drawer. A common size for the screws is 8-32 x 1" (25mm). This will allow the screw to pass through a ¾" (19mm)-thick drawer front and go ¼" (6mm) into the handle or pull.

If a handle has two machine screws, the distance between the screws (center of one screw to the center of the other) will be a standardized dimension. Traditionally, this was 3" (76mm). However, it is common for handles to have screws that are 3½" (89mm), 3¾" (95mm), and even 4" (102mm) or more apart. The distance between the screw holes in the handles in our kitchen is 5" (127mm).

It is essential to get all of the handles and pulls lined up, level, and even (**Figure 6-81**). Otherwise, the drawers and doors may appear to be uneven or unlevel when actually they are not. For attaching door handles, I like to use a shop-built drilling jig whenever possible to keep things consistent and even. Many handles and pulls leave little room for error when drilling and aligning the

holes because there is often little material to overlap the hole. A jig like the one pictured here will solve this problem when mounting door handles and it will also make the drilling go much faster (**Figure 6-82**).

Most drawers are made using a wooden box with a separate face mounted to the front (**Figure 6-86**). This makes it possible for the manufacturer to make a limited range of drawers and then cover them with an almost unlimited variety of fronts. As I mentioned above, most pulls and handles come with screws only long enough to go through one layer of wood (1" [25mm]), in this case the drawer front. One solution to this problem is to buy screws long enough to pass through both the drawer front and the front of the drawer box (1½" to 1¾" [38mm to 44mm] long).

Another solution is to remove the drawer front, apply the pull, and remount the drawer front to the box. The main advantage to this approach is ease in aligning the other drawer fronts independent of the pulls.

Figure 6-81. Align the drawer pulls horizontally and mount the door handles at the same height.

Figure 6-86. A box with a separate face mounted to its front with a couple of screws comprises a typical drawer.

QUICK TIP

Before removing the drawer front from the drawer box, make a registration mark on the back of the drawer front to make it easy to reattach the drawer in the same position.

To do this, remove the face of each drawer by loosening the screws inside the box (**Figure 6-87**). Then, lay out the holes and double check their spacing to make sure they line up with the pull (**Figure 6-88**).

Now drill the holes for the mounting screws through the drawer front (**Figure 6-89**). There is still a little problem here. The screw head will keep the drawer front from pulling up tight against the drawer box. To solve this problem, I used a spade bit the size of the screw head to create a countersunk hole (**Figures 6-90** and **6-91**). Then attach the pull to the front with the mounting screws coming in from the back (**Figure 6-92**) . Finally, reattach the drawer front in its original position (**Figure 6-93**).

Figure 6-87. Start by unscrewing the drawer front from the drawer box.

Figure 6-88. Next lay out the holes and use a pull to check that the spacing is correct. You can also build an alignment jig as explained in the *Tips from the Trades* box on page 130.

Figure 6-89. Drill the screw holes in the drawer front the same size as the screws.

Figure 6-90. Then, turn the face over and use a larger bit to drill down about ⅛" (3mm) to create countersinks on the back face.

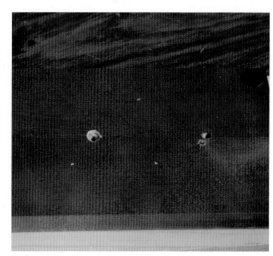

Figure 6-91. The countersinks make a recessed space for the screw head.

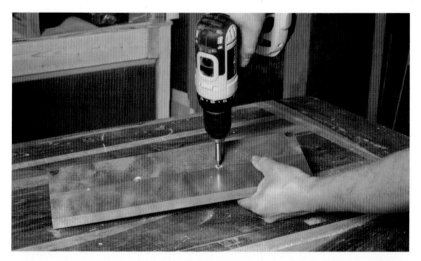

Figure 6-92. Next, attach the pull with the two screws driven in from the back.

Figure 6-93. Finally, reattach the drawer front to the drawer box.

CHAPTER 7

Countertops

At one time, the standard material for kitchen countertops was Formica, usually in harvest gold. Things have changed and there is a variety of choices, including materials, colors, and price ranges from which you can choose. The important thing is to consider function as well as appearance in your choice.

I like to consider two things in deciding what material to use. First, how easy is it to clean up? Wiping down kitchen countertops is a chore you may perform many times a day. Porous surfaces or those with wide grout seams collect dirt and germs easily.

The second item is durability and longevity. Will it stand up to the abuse of cutting on it, placing hot pots on it, rolling out dough, and all of the other daily tasks you will perform in your kitchen? Newer countertops such as granite, ceramic tile, and even concrete often withstand intense use better than some traditional countertop materials.

PRICING AND PROS/CONS

The cost of a countertop can be one of the major expenses in a new or remodeled kitchen. Fortunately, today the selection is wider and you can get a beautiful, durable countertop—without breaking the bank.

Usually specified by the lineal or square foot, countertop surfaces run from $10 per linear foot to $200 per square foot. So a typical 200 square foot kitchen that has 30 linear feet of countertop (approximately 90 square feet with backsplash) might run anywhere from $300 to more than $15,000. Be sure to find out from your dealer if this includes creating a template to match your kitchen's needs, delivery, and installation (if you are not going to do it yourself). Of course, prices will vary depending upon the color, pattern, texture, edging detail (ogees, bullnoses, etc.), custom widths, and number of seams and holes (such as for sinks.)

Be aware that many countertops are pre-fabricated in a factory so exact measurements are critical. Be sure the dealer actually comes to your site to take measurements and makes a template. In addition, removal of the existing countertop may or may not be included in the price. However, this is not an issue if you are totally remodeling your kitchen as you have already removed the countertops at the same time you removed the old cabinets.

Finally, if you are not going to install your own countertops, get several estimates, and ask for references, length of experience, and whether the installer is properly bonded, insured, and licensed. You can also always get more information about the dealer or installer from your Better Business Bureau.

GRANITE AND GRANITE TILE

The gold standard for countertops today is granite. It defines elegance and will make any kitchen, no matter how modest, look more beautiful. Available in almost 3,000 colors, it will definitely add significant value to a home. Until recently, the cost of a granite countertop ($175 a square foot and up) was a large portion of the budget for a new kitchen. The cost has come down a bit because of a few recent developments

Traditionally, granite was ¾" (19mm) thick. This was too thin visually for most applications so the local granite shop had to glue a lip of matching granite around the outer edge of the counter. Then the edge required shaping. Cutting and shipping granite in a thickness of about 1¼" (31mm) eliminates the edge lamination process at the local shop. There is also new technology for cutting, shaping, and polishing the granite that speeds up the process and lowered the cost.

Granite tile has always been a less expensive option, but until recently, it was only available in 12" by 12" (305mm by 305mm) squares that sold for about $7.50 to $10 each. The smaller tiles, however, just did not have the visual impact or functionality of a solid granite surface.

Granite tile takes any kitchen to a higher level of elegance.

[SPECIAL TERM]

Ogee: *A double curve with the shape of an elongated S used on the edge of a counter or piece of wood.*

[SPECIAL TERM]

Bullnose: *An edge profile almost rounded over.*

Granite is now available in 24" by 24" (610mm by 610mm) squares that more closely resemble solid granite. Most kitchen counters are 24" (610mm) deep, thus minimizing the cutting and grouting of seams (**Figure 7-1**). I used the 24" (610mm) squares in our kitchen and they cost $66 each or about $16.49 per square foot. The granite tiles are 14mm thick (about 9⁄16"), which allows anyone who has access to a rented tile saw to cut them.

**Solid Granite Cost Per Square Foot:
$60 to $175 (includes installation,
a plain edge, and a few hole cuts)**

**Granite Tile Cost Per Square Foot:
$7.50 to $20**

Figure 7-1. In our kitchen, I used 24" (610mm) squares that closely resemble solid granite and edged them with wood trim. For more on the installation, see page 152.

RESTAURANT LESSONS FROM A PRO
Working on Granite

Pastry chefs love granite counters because they are very smooth, which helps to keep dough from sticking to the countertop. Granite counters also remain relatively cool, which helps keep the dough firm by preventing the butter in the dough from melting and softening. To increase the benefit, during construction, install refrigerant coils under the area of the counter intended for working dough. An alternative method is to place a bag or bowl of ice in the area before working the dough. Marble works as a pastry slab in small areas, but is generally too soft for most kitchen counters.

Pros:

- Appearance. Each slab is unique

- Adds visual and financial value to a home

- Durable. Will last a lifetime

- Heat, scratch, and dent resistant

- Remains cool for pastry work

- Granite tiles are now available for easy DIY installation and low cost

Cons:

- Solid granite is expensive (thin tiles are lower cost)

- Expensive to add edge profiles to solid granite (simple bevels, ogee, bullnose)

- Requires sealing to avoid stains

- Requires special cleaners as household cleaners may damage the surface

- Can crack if something heavy is dropped on it

- Professional installation is required (unless using tiles)

QUICK TIP

If you use granite tile that is only 15mm thick, install wood (as I did) or granite edging that is available separately from your tile dealer.

ENGINEERED STONE

Engineered stone is not solid stone but uses the latest technology to combine particles of natural stone, granite, and 93% quartz with polymers and epoxy. It has a brilliant, nonporous 1¼" (32mm)-thick surface with one big advantage—it costs less than solid granite.

In addition, engineered stone is available in more colors than granite and resists wear and chemicals. It is also heat, stain, and scratch resistant. It is easy to maintain without the annual sealing required of natural stone. One of the advantages of engineered stone is the color and patterns are much more uniform than granite, so you are more likely to know the exact color you will get. In addition, if you want to add counter space later, you can order the same color and shade.

Some of the brand names of engineered stone include DuPont Zodiaq, LG Viatera, Cambria Quartz, and Silestone. One national franchise, Granite Transformations (*www. GraniteTransformations.com*) offers Trend Stone and Trend Glass, a fusion of transparent tempered glass and stone fragments. They can build a countertop that will sit right over an existing countertop for a clean, one-day installation.

Engineered Stone Cost Per Square Foot: $40 to $125+

Pros:

- Appearance (stone look)
- Color and pattern more uniform than granite
- Adds visual and financial value to a home
- Extremely non-porous
- Twice as strong as granite
- Heat, scratch, stain, and dent resistant
- Maintenance free: does not require annual sealing
- Edge profiles ranging from simple bevels and bullnose to ogee

Cons:

- High cost
- Heavier than granite
- Professional installation required

Photo courtesy of Granite Transformations.

Engineered stone is another option for consideration in designing your new kitchen.

CERAMIC TILE

Ceramic tile offers advantages other materials do not, as well as cost savings.

Ceramic Tile Cost Per Square Foot:
$5 to $15 for simple solid colors;
$20 to $100 for patterned tiles

Pros:

- Standard tiles are lower-cost option
- Offered in range of colors, textures and designs
- Cleans easily
- Withstands hot pans
- Installable by most homeowners

Cons:

- Counter surface is uneven
- Tiles chip or crack easily
- Grout lines can become stained and gather food and crumbs
- Grout lines need periodic sealing to repel moisture
- Not hygienic
- Custom-designed tiles usually expensive

QUICK TIP

Some types of tile used in bathrooms are too soft for the rigors of a kitchen counter. Consult the salesperson before selecting any tile for a kitchen.

Ceramic tile is another great option for countertops. It is available in a tremendous variety of shapes, sizes, and colors. Because it is installed a section at a time, it is easy for most people to learn how to cut and install. Tile saws are usually available to rent at tile supply stores and home centers. You will also have to learn how to grout between the tiles (*more on that later*).

The advantages of tile are twofold. First, it can be inexpensive as even high-end tile will not cost as much as a solid granite or engineered stone countertop. Another advantage of tile is the visual aspect. Tile is available in a range of colors and patterns, and cuts easily into an array of shapes.

PLASTIC LAMINATE

For the second half of the twentieth century, plastic laminate became the most common countertop material used in American homes. Many people call it Formica, but that is one of many brand names of plastic laminate. Others include Wilsonart and Nevamar. Layers of paper treated with a plastic resin and pressed together under high heat and pressure comprise plastic laminate. Providing a smooth, but thin surface, plastic laminates are the most inexpensive materials for kitchen countertops. Available in a variety of colors and patterns from lumberyards and plywood dealers, they can also be among the easiest countertop option to install.

Purchase plastic laminate in sheets as big as 60" by 144" (1,524mm by 3,658mm) and cover large areas without seams. Glue sheets down to a particleboard or medium density fiberboard (MDF) substrate and cover the edge of the counter with the same material, or, for a more attractive counter, with solid wood.

Home improvement centers also offer molded plastic laminate counter tops called post-formed countertops. Some of these are quite long and are available with a 45° corner and hardware for joining the corners together (**Figure 7-2**).

[SPECIAL TERM]

Post-formed countertop: *A wood-based countertop with plastic laminate already applied. The countertop has a built-in backsplash on the back. It also includes a large lip extending past the backsplash that is scribable to make it conform to a wall. Most also have a molded edge or bump on the front with a lip to prevent water on the counter from running off onto the floor.*

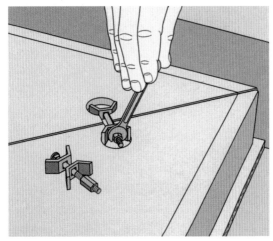

Figure 7-2. Use special hardware that fits into the bottom face of a wood-based countertop to hold together 45° corners.

Plastic Laminate Cost Per Square Foot: $10 to $45 installed or $12 to $15 (linear foot) in post-formed countertop as a do-it-yourself project.

Pros:

- Low cost
- Easy to clean
- Many colors and designs
- Easy to maintain
- Can be made and installed by a homeowner with some basic power tools (table saw, router, etc.)

Cons:

- Scratches, chips, and stains are almost impossible to repair
- Seams show
- Cover required for front edge and ends. (Front ends exempt if purchased as post-formed countertop.)
- Excessive heat (hot pans) causes damage
- Water under the laminate damages and swells the wood chip substrate

Plastic laminate offers some advantages over other countertop materials, while being the most inexpensive material available.

SOLID SURFACE

Solid surface plastic countertops are an excellent choice for designs emphasizing curved edges without seams.

Solid Surface Cost Per Square Foot: $40 to $90

Pros:

• Variety of colors and patterns

• Seamless

• Stain resistant

• Durable

• Variety of edging and border options

• Can form integral sink

• Easy to remove scratches

Cons:

• Moderately expensive

• Somewhat vulnerable to hot pans

• Requires professional installation

Another type of plastic countertop falls under the title solid surface. The most common brand name is Corian, and, like Formica for plastic laminates, Kleenex for facial tissues, or Xerox for all paper copies, some people mistakenly call the whole category Corian. However, there are other brand names such as Avonite, Swanstone, Gibraltor, and Earthstone.

This thick plastic material can be shaped and formed making it ideal for use with inset sinks and designs that emphasize smooth curved edges without seams. Solid surface countertops also can incorporate a built-in seamless backsplash. Though they cost more than plastic laminates they have a much cleaner look. They also take specialized tools to cut, shape, and smooth, so homeowner installation is uncommon.

One advantage of solid surface countertops is they are a consistent color all of the way through. Scratches are sandable and profiles cut into the edges will be uniform in color.

WOOD

Though wood primarily is a secondary countertop material in a kitchen, it offers advantages over other materials.

Wood Cost Per Square Foot: $30 to $125

Pros:

• Cleans easily

• Smooth

• Easily sanded and resealed if damaged

• Withstands cutting and chopping without damaging knives

• Installable by a homeowner with some basic tools.

Cons:

• Damaged by water (keep away from sink)

• Not stain resistant

• Requires regular maintenance (oiling or sealing)

• Subject to surface burns by hot pans

An entire kitchen featuring wooden countertops is an option, but smaller areas for cutting, such as a butcher block, are more common. Maple is the most commonly used type of wood for countertops because it is hard and it will not react to most foods placed on it. Some woods such as walnut contain oils and organic compounds such as tannins that will react with certain foods, leaving stains on the counter and affecting the taste of the food and the color of the wood. If you plan on wood, consult a reference book on different types of woods before choosing a wood for a kitchen countertop.

Bacterial build up on wood is a common misconception. Actually, wood is one of the more sanitary products for the kitchen with inherent properties that protect it from bacteria.

Of course, wood is relatively inexpensive and easy to work with and install. Sanding and refinishing are easy. On bare, unfinished wood, I would recommend treating it with mineral oil or walnut oil on a regular basis, especially near the sink.

CAST CONCRETE

Recently, cast concrete has become popular for kitchen countertops, especially in kitchens with a contemporary design. It can be tinted with various colors of pigment and inset with tile, wood, or any meaningful object. The real advantage is it forms to virtually any shape including curves and undulations. It can be ground, polished, stamped, or textured to be as rough as stone or as smooth as glass. Covering vertical surfaces with concrete such as an island base, the exposed end of a cabinet, or backsplashes can create more unity.

With enough added support, concrete countertops also can be any thickness (usually 1" to 1½" [25mm to 38mm]). Concrete weighs about the same as granite. Manufacture of concrete countertops takes place in a controlled factory setting using a mold.

One of the best sources for information about concrete countertops, including information for do-it-yourselfers, is *www.concreteexchange.com*.

Cast Concrete Cost Per Square Foot: $60 to $150

Pros:

- Made to just about any shape, size, or thickness

- Heat and scratch resistant. (Note: Although concrete itself may be heat and scratch resistant, the type of sealer applied may not be. Be sure to review manufacturer instructions to be certain of product requirements.)

- Exotic and unusual in appearance

- Infinite range of colors

- Eco-friendly

Cons:

- Expensive due to custom work and processing time

- Possible cracking if not properly cured or handled

- Porous if left unsealed. (Depending on the type of cast concrete and topical sealers you use, the concrete may or may not require regular resealing. Be sure to review manufacturer instructions to be certain of product requirements.)

- Professional manufacturing and installation recommended

QUICK TIP

The concrete used for countertops is highly engineered and every fabricator has a different formula. It is not the same concrete used for a sidewalk or driveway!

Photo courtesy of Trueform Concrete, www.trueformconcrete.com.

Cast concrete is gaining popularity as a countertop material and offers an exotic look and feel among its advantages.

STAINLESS STEEL

Though its most common use is in commercial kitchens, stainless steel is another option to consider for your kitchen project.

Stainless Steel Cost Per Square Foot: $85 to $200

Pros:

- Easiest to clean
- Heat resistant
- Stain resistant
- Can roll dough on it
- Can form integral sink or any shape and dimension desired

Cons:

- Expensive
- Noisy (unless attached to appropriate substrate)
- May dent
- You cannot cut on it
- Shows scratches and fingerprints
- Requires special tools for fabrication

Stainless steel is the most common countertop material for restaurant kitchens because it is nonporous, easy to quickly clean, and will not react with the combination of bleach and water commonly used to clean and disinfect them—often many times in a single night.

Stainless steel's industrial appearance may not look appropriate for the countertops for an entire home kitchen, but it can be an excellent choice for a small heavily used area or an area designated for meat cutting. Manufactured to your specifications, stainless steel comes in just about any width and length providing a seamless countertop.

Some of the newer applications include brushed or textured finishes, which help camouflage scratches and fingerprints. Standard finishes are bullnose, rolled, and marine (no drip). Use thinner 16-gauge stainless steel in home kitchens and 14- and 12-gauge stainless steel in restaurant kitchens.

QUICK TIP

Don't be surprised to see more kitchens designed with other metals such as bronze, copper, zinc, and even pewter. Each has its own unique look and characteristics. For more on using these metals for countertops go to *www. BrooksCustom.com.*

RESTAURANT LESSONS FROM A PRO
Clean Up

Ease of clean up is an important factor in both the professional kitchen and home kitchen. It saves time and reduces cross contamination of foods. Smooth surfaces such as granite, Corian® some types of plastic laminates, and stainless steel are best for easy clean up, while uneven or porous surfaces make it difficult to fully remove food pathogens.

Something as simple as having too little counter space near the refrigerator could be a food safety problem, as people often take several items out of the refrigerator at once. If this counter space overlaps with a meat preparation area or near a sink typically filled with dirty dishes, the potential for cross contamination increases.

Professional kitchens (and increasingly home kitchens) use stainless steel surfaces and appliances because they are easy to clean and stand up to bleach and other chemicals used to sanitize them on a regular basis. (Note: Some new cleaners have a small amount of bleach in them. It's usually enough to kill bacteria but not enough to damage countertops made of natural stone, laminates, or tile.)

Also important is having adequate access to faucets for hand washing and food preparation. If all food preparation is done in one crowded space and more than one person is involved, it may be difficult for individuals to wash their hands before helping to prepare foods, or after handling raw meat. Alternatively, if the food preparation area is too far from a sink, proper handling of food and sanitation become difficult.

This kitchen especially designed for catering has almost all surfaces covered with stainless steel, which cleans easily after every job is complete.

In a large commercial kitchen such as this one, it is important for sanitation that stainless steel sinks are available near the food preparation area.

COUNTERTOP HEIGHT

Today's kitchen is the activity center of many homes, used to prepare family meals, bake, preserve fruits and vegetables, eat quick meals, and even as workspaces and offices. Each of these activities might best be suited to a different height counter and a different surface material. The traditional 36" (914mm)-high matching countertop look is disappearing and people are selecting a mixture of colors, textures, and heights. Some examples of different work zones and their needs include:

FOOD PREPARATION AREA

- 27" (686mm)-high drop-down counter for mixing and beating

- Wood chopping block

- Stainless steel preparation area for meat cutting

- Integrated sink allows for cleaning of fruits and vegetables and easy disposal of scraps

- Raised metal strips set into the countertop for hot pans

BAKING AREA

- Lower countertops for kneading and rolling dough (7 to 8 inches [178mm to 203mm] below the elbow)

- Granite or marble countertops

ENTERTAINMENT AREA

- Higher countertops accommodating tall stools, buffet-style serving, or snacking spaces

- Dramatic look of granite, engineered stone, or colorful solid surface

OFFICE AREA

- 30" to 34" (762mm to 864mm)-high counters with adequate knee space

- Pull-out computer keyboard tray with keyboard height approximately equal to seated elbow height (28" to 30" [711mm to 762mm])

- Warm, inviting feel (i.e. wood or colored plastic rather than granite)

COUNTERTOP AND BACKSPLASH INSTALLATION

Even if you are having your countertops made or cut by someone else, you may be able to save some money and time by laying down a base for the countertop yourself. Ask your countertop manufacturer if you can do the prep work and what kind of a base he would recommend.

PLYWOOD BASE

Many of the countertop materials described earlier in this chapter require placing a layer of plywood over the top of the cabinets. The plywood acts both as a base under the finished countertops and reinforces the cabinets by further tying them together. In most cases, an exterior grade of plywood is required to better resist moisture.

The first step is to determine the exact width to cut the plywood. The average countertop is about 24" (610mm) deep plus any trim or edge that runs along the front. You will also need to consider the thickness of a backsplash when calculating the exact depth of your counters and whether the backsplash is going to sit on top of the countertop or behind it (refer to Figure 4-10 on page 85 as a reference).

Ceramic or granite countertop tiles generally come in sizes that easily add up to 24" (610mm) without cutting (6" by 6" [152mm by 152mm], 12" by 12" [305mm by 305mm], and 24" by 24" [610mm by 610mm] are common). Lay out some tiles and measure them to calculate the *exact* width of the plywood. Be sure to factor in the spaces (grout lines) between each row of tiles when adding this up. For my project, I used 1/16" (4mm) veneer scraps as spacers (**Figure 7-3**).

To finish calculating the depth (width) of the plywood base for the countertop, determine

Figure 7-3. The granite tiles I used measured 24" x 24" (610mm by 610mm) and I used 1/16" (2mm) veneer scraps as spacers.

the type of lip or border for the front. A border will overlap the face of the cabinets somewhat to prevent spilled liquids from running off the countertop and down the face of the cabinets. Manufactured cabinets are often 23¾" (603mm) deep. Rip a 48" (1,219mm) wide sheet of plywood in half down the center and each half will be just less than 24" (610mm) wide after accounting for the thickness of the saw blade. In many cases, this is a good depth for the countertop base. Even if there is a thick border around the countertop, the plywood base should be proud of the cabinet face about ¼" (6mm). The border should overlap the plywood base on the underside by at least ⅛" (3mm). This will hide the plywood and cover any irregularities along the top edge of the cabinets.

Attach the plywood base from both the underside and the top. It will be easiest to attach the plywood from the top first to prevent it from

QUICK TIP
Have your tiles on hand before you start cutting the plywood so that you know their exact measurements. While you are at the store, also pick up some plastic spacers that will determine the width of your grout lines.

Figure 7-4. Adding 2 x 4 blocking behind the lazy Susan units in the corners provides support and a surface for screwing down the plywood. Be sure the blocking is level with the top of the cabinets.

Figure 7-5. Screw down through the top of the plywood and into the face frame in the front and blocking or cabinet sides in the back.

shifting while drilling from the bottom. This may require some extra blocking in the corners or other areas where the cabinets do not reach the back wall (**Figure 7-4**).

In the front, use screws to attach the plywood to the face frames (**Figure 7-5**). Attach strips of plywood around the sink opening and up to the edge of any appliances as well (**Figure 7-6**).

Most cabinets will have some type of blocks, strips, or triangular gussets near the top for holding the corners together and attaching the countertop from underneath. My cabinets had gussets, but as I tightened down a screw to hold the top in place, the gusset started to bend and break (**Figure 7-7**).

To solve the problem I placed a scrap block of wood the proper thickness between the gusset and the plywood top. In addition, I pre-drilled a hole through the gusset and the scrap block (**Figure 7-8**), and used a pan head screw to prevent the screw from digging into the wood (**Figure 7-9**). Continue this process around the kitchen covering all of the cabinets with plywood (**Figure 7-10**).

QUICK TIP

Countersink the screw heads below the surface of the plywood so the countertop material will lay level.

Figure 7-6. Cut narrow strips of plywood as needed to fit around the sink or any special openings in the countertop.

Figure 7-7. As I tried to tighten a screw through the corner gusset and into the plywood, the particleboard gusset started to bend and almost broke.

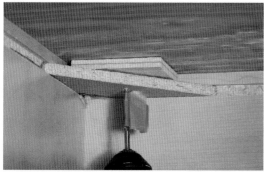

Figure 7-8. Pre-drill a screw hole through the gusset and the scrap block. Note the masking tape on the drill bit as a depth gauge. I wanted to drill the hole just deep enough to pass through the gusset and the block. The screw will then grab into the plywood only and pull it down onto the top of the cabinet.

Figure 7-9. Now screw through the pre-drilled hole and into the bottom of the plywood.

TILE BACKER

If you plan on using tile as a countertop material, apply a moisture barrier. Several types of materials block moisture, prevent mold and mildew, and create a flat surface to properly secure the tile. A backer is required for many countertop materials. Some manufacturers void warranties if a backer is not used.

The traditional material to use for a tile baker is cement board, which is a composite material with great structural integrity (**Figure 7-11**). Cut cement board using a saw with a composite blade, or score and cut like drywall. Cement board may require a carbide-cutting tool for scoring because it can dull a knife quickly.

I used a material similar to cement board called DenShield, a gypsum-based product that is as easy to cut as drywall, but offers many of the same properties as cement board. It has a fiberglass-matt facing and a unique acrylic coating. To cut cement board or DenShield, lay a straightedge on

Figure 7-10. Apply the plywood base to the top of all of the counters and then move on to the next step.

Figure 7-11. Cut cement board, which is typically ½" (13mm) thick, in the same manner as you would drywall.

Figure 7-12. Lay down the cement board or DenShield on the floor and score it with a sharp utility knife.

the cut line and score it with a knife (**Figure 7-12**). Then stand the panel up and bend it along the cut line to snap it (**Figure 7-13**). Use a sharp knife to cut through the other side (**Figure 7-14**), and a drywall saw to cut around a detail (**Figure 7-15** and **7-16**).

Figure 7-13. Stand the scored panel up on edge and snap it toward you for a clean cut.

Figure 7-14. Use the utility knife to cut it clean through from the other side.

Figure 7-15. Use a simple drywall saw to cut around details and corners.

Figure 7-16. While exercising patience, cut the backer to fit around a molding on the adjacent cabinet.

After cutting the backer to size, attach it to the top of the plywood to create a flat surface. I like to use a latex Portland cement mortar for a strong bond. A stirring bit on the end of a drill will help to speed up the process (**Figure 7-17**). After allowing the chemicals in the cement to react with the water for a few minutes, apply an even coat of cement to the plywood with a ¼" (6mm) notched trowel (**Figure 7-18**). Then lower the backer gently onto the plywood (**Figure 7-19**). Finally, attach the backer with galvanized or exterior grade bugle head screws making sure the backer does not overlap the plywood along the edge (**Figure 7-20**).

Figure 7-17. Mix the mortar with the correct amount of water as described on the bag.

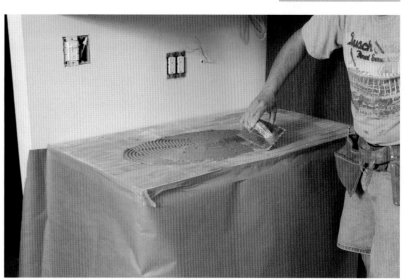

Figure 7-18. Spread an even coat of mortar all the way to the edges using a notched trowel.

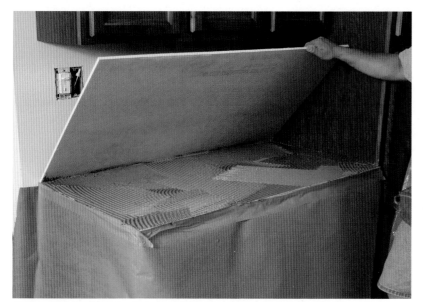

Figure 7-19. Place the backer carefully into position on top of the cement-covered plywood.

Figure 7-20. Screw the backer down to the plywood with screws every 8" to 10" (203mm to 254mm) making sure the screw heads sit slightly below the surface of the backer.

TILES

After the backer is firmly in place, add the tiles. For our kitchen, I chose 24" by 24" (610mm by 610mm) granite tiles, so there was not a lot of cutting necessary. Nearly every project requires some cutting to get everything to fit, so I rented a tile saw that was wide enough to cut the 24" (610mm) tiles (**Figure 7-21**).

To save time on the rental fee, place the tiles into a pleasing pattern and do your planning before you rent the saw. I always buy a few extra tiles because some inevitably break. Start from the corner and work out away from it. If you work toward the corner you may end up having to cut some of the tiles to fit and the result could be an uneven corner.

Attach the tiles with Portland cement in the same manner as when applying the backer to the plywood. When setting the tiles in place, use commercially-available spacers or strips of wood that are of the same thickness to get a consistent grout line (**Figure 7-22**). Use a level or straightedge to ensure the tiles are flat (**Figure 7-23**). The cement should be soft enough to shift the tiles for about 10 minutes. Allow the cement to set at least 24 hours before placing anything heavy on the counter or applying the grout.

Figure 7-21. Using a rented tile saw with a blade embedded with industrial diamonds, I cut the granite tile to size. A slow steady cut works best because otherwise the blade wanders. There will be a lot of water spills and sprays from the saw, so consider cutting outside.

Figure 7-22. I use scraps of veneer from my shop as spacers to keep a consistent grout line.

Figure 7-23. Check for flatness. To get the tiles even, tap the tiles with a rubber mallet or your hand.

BACKSPLASHES

A backsplash is a border around the back of a counter that protects the wall and keeps moisture from getting down behind the counter. Most often, the material selected for a backsplash will either match or complement the countertop material. Use decorative tiles to add a splash of color in the backsplash. If using granite tiles or unglazed ceramic tiles (which generally have a matte finish), the tiles must be sealed. (If you are using a post-formed plastic laminate counter, you can add an additional decorative tile border above the backsplash that is a part of the counter.)

For our kitchen, we chose smaller granite tile that matched the countertop. The tile shipped in square sheets in rows of 4" by 4" (102mm by 102mm) tiles backed with fiberglass mesh (**Figure 7-24**), which made it easier to install with fewer spacers. Cut the mesh apart with a utility knife (**Figure 7-25**).

There are a couple of options for attaching the backsplash tile to the wall. If the wall is drywall, score it first with a knife and attach the tile directly to the wall. A second method is to attach a tile backer to the wall first and then cement the tiles to the backer (**Figure 7-26**). After the Portland cement mix for the vertical tile has set for a few minutes, apply the tiles (**Figure 7-27**). Continue to check the vertical tiles for shifting as gravity may cause them to move.

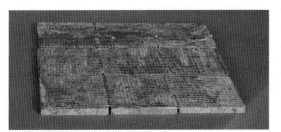

Figure 7-24. Tiles attached with fiberglass-mesh backing make the job of consistently spacing the tiles much easier.

Figure 7-25. Use a utility knife or box cutter to cut the tiles apart as needed before attaching them to the wall.

Figure 7-26. Here you can see I have attached a strip of tile backer to the adjacent wooden cabinet, but just scored the drywall at the back of the counter. Then, I applied the cement directly to both surfaces with a notched trowel.

Figure 7-27. Apply the tiles and let the cement set. Note the small scraps of veneer I put under each tile to form a uniform grout line between the countertop and the backsplash.

Adding a Decorative Mosaic

One of the first things people comment on when they enter our new kitchen is the unique decorative mosaic pattern I created over the stove (**Figure 7-28**). It was actually quite easy to design, added only about $100 in expense, and serves two purposes. First, its mosaic pattern is decorative. But, second, it provides an easily cleanable surface to handle grease splatters. A pattern like this is a good place to bring in materials of contrasting colors and have a little fun experimenting with different shapes.

Once you have an idea, the best place to start is a full sized drawing on a piece of paper or wood (**Figure 7-29**). As you cut them, place the tiles right on the drawing (**Figure 7-30**). When you are satisfied with the appearance, transfer the main parts of the drawing to the wall (**Figure 7-31**).

Start attaching the tiles to the wall using the same method as you did with the backsplash (**Figure 7-32**). After attaching all of the tiles to the wall, the pattern is ready for some wood trim and grout (**Figure 7-33**).

Figure 7-28. A decorative wall mosaic above the cook top can add a dramatic touch to just about any kitchen.

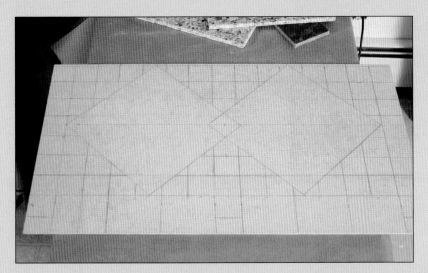

Figure 7-29. I like to draw out my design with a pencil on a piece of plywood or hardboard.

Figure 7-30. Place the tiles in their final position on the pattern.

Figure 7-31. Next, as a reference, draw the main parts of the drawing right on the wall.

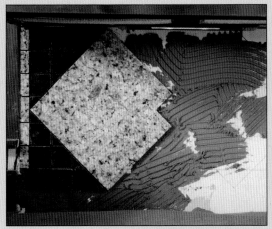

Figure 7-32. Use Portland cement or a similar product to attach the tiles to the wall. Monitor the tiles and be sure they do not slide downward before they start to dry.

Figure 7-33. Allow the tiles to dry 24 hours before applying the grout.

Wood biscuit: *A thin, football-shaped piece of wood that fits into openings cut into two joining boards. Cut biscuit openings with a special tool called a biscuit (or plate) joiner. This provides both alignment and some strength to the joint.*

Figure 7-34. Wood trim added around the countertop dresses up and protects the edges. It should overhang the bottom face of the plywood by at least ⅛" to hide the plywood. Join the corners with miter joints.

Figure 7-35. Add wood trim around the backsplash and decorative wall tile.

QUICK TIP

Apply finished wood trim before grouting the tile to fill space between the wood trim and the tiles with grout. It also prevents the stain and finish applied to the wood from damaging the tile or the grout.

Figure 7-36. Mix grout powder (in can at left) with water and apply with a grout float (center). Matching grout is also available in a tube for sealing around sinks and hard to reach areas.

TRIM

Tile usually has a rough, unfinished edge. To dress it up, I like to add wood trim around the counters (**Figure 7-34**) and the backsplash (**Figure 7-35**). (Note: Some purchased ceramic tiles have smooth, rounded edges. Others have special ceramic edging pieces. Either type negates the need for wood trim.) I used maple stained to match the color of the cabinets and sealed with a couple of coats of polyurethane. After cutting the trim to size, I attached it to the edge of the counters with glue and nails. (Wood biscuits are another option for attaching the trim.) I later filled the nail holes with matching filler. To attach the wood trim to the wall around the backsplash, I used Liquid Nails construction adhesive.

GROUT

Grout fills the spaces between the tiles and the tile and wood trim. Epoxy grout is the best grout to help resist stains.

Two common forms of grout—a powder mixed with water or in a tube and applied just like caulk (**Figure 7-36**)—work well for kitchen counters and backsplashes. The fastest way to grout a kitchen is to mix the powder grout with water, apply it to the seams with a pastry bag, and then level it out with a grout float. Some grout may work better with an *add mix* added to it. Consult the label on your grout can or bag.

To grout the tile, begin by placing grout over the seams (**Figure 7-37**). Then tilt the grout float at an angle to the seam and push along the length of the seam (**Figure 7-38**). Allow the caulk to dry for a few minutes then wipe the surface with a clean sponge to remove any excess grout.

Most types of grout will require a sealer, but you should allow the grout to set 24 to 48 hours before it is sealed. Do not wait too long because unsealed grout can stain easily.

Ask your tile dealer if the granite, natural stone, or ceramic tile you are using also requires a sealer. There are sealers that will seal both the tile and the grout. A good quality sealer for natural stone costs up to $50 a pint, but is worth the expense to seal the material and prevent stains. There are also maintenance products available that clean and seal at the same time. These will help your finished countertops look clean and new for years to come (**Figure 7-39**).

Figure 7-38. When removing the excess grout from the surface of the tiles, always hold the float at an angle to the seam.

Figure 7-37. Work the grout right down into the seam with the grout float. Be sure there are not any gaps.

QUICK TIP

There is a variety of grout colors from which to choose. Choosing one that is similar in colors to the tile creates a more unified look. Note: Lighter colored grouts are not as effective at hiding dirt.

[SPECIAL TERM]

Grout float: A tool with a handle and foam rubber base used to gently force grout into the seams between the tiles and remove it from the surface of the tiles.

QUICK TIP

After applying the grout, spray it with distilled water periodically for the next 12 to 24 hours to prevent it from drying too fast and cracking. Covering the countertop with plastic for 24 hours keeps it moist.

Figure 7-39. A well-maintained countertop will add beauty and value to your home's kitchen for years to come.

More Great Project Books from Fox Chapel Publishing

Tree Craft
35 Rustic Projects that Bring the Outdoors In
By Chris Lubkemann

Beautify your home with rustic accents made from twigs and branches. More than 35 eco-chic projects for a coat rack, curtain rods, candle holders, desk sets, picture frames, a table and more.

ISBN: 978-1-56523-455-0
$19.95 • 128 Pages

Foolproof Wood Finishing
For Those Who Love to Build & Hate to Finish
By Teri Masaschi

Take the mystery out of finishing and avoid costly mistakes with easy-to-follow exercises designed by woodworking's premier finishing instructor. Also includes 20 recipies for classic looks and amusing "adventures in finishing" anecdotes.

ISBN: 978-1-56523-303-4
$19.95 • 200 Pages

Traditional American Rooms
Celebrating Style, Craftsmanship, and Historic Woodwork
By Brent Hull

Immerse yourself in the elegance and character of historic American architecture with this guide to the magnificent millwork of the Winterthur Museum and Country Estate.

ISBN: 978-1-56523-322-5
$35.00 • 200 Pages

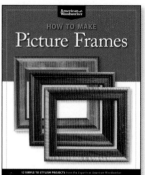

How to Make Picture Frames
12 Simple to Stylish Projects from the Experts at American Woodworker
Edited by Randy Johnson

Add a special touch to cherished photos or artwork with hand-made picture frames. The experts at *American Woodworker* give step-by-step instructions using a variety of woods and styles.

ISBN: 978-1-56523-459-8
$19.95 • 120 Pages

Illustrated Cabinetmaking
How to Design & Construct Furniture that Works
By William H. Hylton

The most complete visual guide to furniture construction ever published! Includes hundreds of drawings and exploded diagrams.

ISBN: 978-1-56523-369-0
$24.95 • 374 Pages

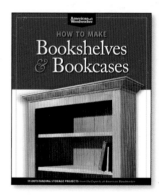

How to Make Bookshelves and Bookcases
19 Outstanding Storage Projects from the Experts at American Woodworker
Edited by Randy Johnson

Build functional yet stylish pieces from a simple wall shelf to a grand bookcase. The experts at *American Woodworker* give step-by-step instructions using various types of wood.

ISBN: 978-1-56523-458-1
$19.95 • 160 Pages

WOODCARVING *ILLUSTRATED*   SCROLLSAW *Woodworking & Crafts*

In addition to being a leading source of woodworking books and DVDs, Fox Chapel also publishes two premiere magazines. Released quarterly, each delivers premium projects, expert tips and techniques from today's finest woodworking artists, and in-depth information about the latest tools, equipment, and materials.

Subscribe Today!
Woodcarving Illustrated: **888-506-6630**
Scroll Saw Woodworking & Crafts: **888-840-8590**
www.FoxChapelPublishing.com

Look for These Books at Your Local Bookstore or Woodworking Retailer
To order direct, call **800-457-9112** or visit *www.FoxChapelPublishing.com*

By mail, please send check or money order + $4.00 per book for S&H to: Fox Chapel Publishing, 1970 Broad Street, East Petersburg, PA 17520